# GENDERSMART®

*Solving the Communication Puzzle
Between Men and Women*

*This book is the property of:*

_____

# Praise for

# GenderSmart®

*"Jane Sanders has written a delightful, enlightening, reader-friendly book that really does solve the communication puzzle between men and women, without alienating either. Everyone will benefit from reading this book!"*

Lisa Fair, Partner, Deloitte & Touche

*"GenderSmart will clear up so many issues for you, even ones didn't know you had! Jane writes very clearly, with compassion and understanding for both genders."*

Keith Bright, founder and President, Bright Design

*"A terrific book! Definitely one to share with friends of both sexes. Jane Sanders has organized tons of fascinating information to help us solve those pesky puzzles and conflicts."*

Nancy Rishagen, Senior Vice President, KCET Television

*"This book is an excellent resource on how men and women receive and process information differently. GenderSmart is chock full of suggestions and examples that will help improve your communications skills with your employees and spouse."*

George Harben, Research Director, SC Dept. of Commerce

*"Even after the first chapter I found myself applying Jane's knowledge to my professional relationships as well as my personal friendships. GenderSmart makes the challenge of interactions easier and fun!"*

Leslie Gockel, Systems Analyst, Save-A-Lot Ltd.

*"Finally, it's here! GenderSmart gives us a unique path to better understanding our differences and delivers concepts for recognition and acceptance of this diversity. I've gained benefit for both my business and personal relationships!"*

Susan Jay Freeman, Interior Designer, ASID

# GenderSmart®

## Solving the Communication Puzzle Between Men and Women

JANE
SANDERS

Full Gallop Press

# GENDERSMART®

Solving The Communication Puzzle
Between Men and Women

Jane Sanders

© Jane Sanders, 2010. Revised 2004, 2006, 2010.
Full Gallop Press

Cover designed by Tracy Perry, Ideas in Motion, Costa Mesa, CA

*To my parents,*

*Paul and Mary Dickerson - my biggest fans,*

*who instilled in me persistence, courage,*

*determination, and hope.*

*To them I send unwavering, immeasurable,*

*and everlasting love and gratitude.*

# CONTENTS

## GENDERSMART®:

*Solving the Communication Puzzle Between Men and Women*

# INTRODUCTION

*"Men and women, women and men. It will never work."*
**Erica Jong**

Do any of these complaints sound familiar? Men are insensitive. Women are too emotional. Men don't listen. Women talk too much. Men interrupt. Women are indecisive. Men don't value women's opinions. Women can't take a joke. Men don't offer enough detail. Women are manipulative. And on and on.

These complaints certainly fall under the category of stereotypes, however, in the case of gender differences, stereotypes stem from generalities. Generally, women are more emotional than men, and generally, men more so than women appear not to listen as well. But when differences cause misperceptions and misunderstandings, complaints are just the tip of the problem iceberg.

The sexes are saturated with, even defined by, many differences. Stereotypical, evolutionary, biological, and social differences, to name a few. Ignoring these very real differences and convincing ourselves they don't exist, even for honorable reasons such as supporting women's equality efforts, only diminishes our ability to deal with them successfully. It's no wonder a "gender gap" exists, especially when it comes to communication. Unlike Erica Jong, however, I believe and know that men and women will work!

Closing the gap or solving this communication puzzle is possible, and certainly desirable as more women start new businesses, move higher within corporate ranks, and seek out equal romantic partnerships. The benefits of improved communication between men and women at work are numerous, including improved recruiting and retention efforts, more effective teamwork, better sales results, more satisfied customers, higher job satisfaction, increased harmony, lower stress, and even fewer sexual harassment problems.

The benefits of improved communication outside of the workplace – with spouses, partners, children, friends, and others – include less conflict and stress, more harmony, and successful, enjoyable relationships.

## How Do We Solve the Puzzle?

How do we increase the effectiveness of our communication with people of the other sex, or with people using the opposite sex communication style? As with most diversity issues, the solution lies primarily in awareness, understanding, and acceptance.

According to Aaron Kipnis, co-director of the Gender Relations Institute in Santa Barbara, California, sexual-harassment programs have increased fear and anxiety, inhibited spontaneity and communication, and distanced men and women. Kipnis suggests strongly a move away from this reactive kind of training toward more proactive, inclusive training that enhances people's understanding of each other. I couldn't have said it better myself.

Avoidance of gender-based communication issues is usually the result of innocent ignorance. Most men aren't as relationship-oriented as most women, so they don't notice communication problems as readily as women do. Because men still hold many of the top positions in corporate America, gender issues at work often aren't adequately addressed.

It is my experience that many of the teamwork and productivity issues in the workplace stem from gender communication style differences, but go unrecognized as such. People automatically label him as a jerk and her as a bitch, simply because they are unfamiliar with these differences and how they impact communication.

Becoming familiar with the many differences between men and women, in a non-threatening and enjoyable way, and understanding that these differences are desirable and that neither gender's style is right or wrong, will eliminate many communication problems. Different behavior and language styles trigger misperceptions and misunderstandings between the opposite sexes. Recognizing that fact goes a long way toward improved communication.

## Why Gender Communication?

The subject of gender differences has always been near and dear to my heart. Why? First of all, I have two brothers. Growing up, I never could figure them out. They seemed so inconsistent with their affection and communication. One minute helping me catch a frog, the next punching me in the arm as I walked unsuspecting around a corner.

Then as a teenager I entered the world of romantic relationships. That's where I really smacked into the puzzle and learned the meaning of communication confusion! My feelings were hurt regularly. I felt as if I were constantly second-guessing my boyfriends, trying to understand where they were coming from. Was he angry and avoiding me, or just temporarily distracted? But the next time I would see him, he thought nothing was wrong. In fact, he wouldn't even remember the conversation. How could he not remember saying that?! Help!

When I graduated from college with a master's degree in business, I plunged into corporate life as a marketing manager for a major Fortune 500 food company. For a time I was the only woman in my division. Gender communication differences were rampant, but this time I had more at stake - like my job. To increase my chances of success, I started paying attention to the nuances. I needed to take the puzzle more seriously and figure out how to solve it in order to beat the odds and move up in the organization.

In the late Eighties, I experienced two major changes: divorce, and a career move into sales in the graphic design industry, with Fortune 500 marketing executives as my target market. Most of my prospects were men. My interest in gender communication differences soared. I wanted to understand these differences for both professional and personal reasons. I made it my mission. And I read everything I could get my hands on. So it's not surprising that gender communication became my favorite topic when I started my professional speaking and training business in 1993.

Since then I've delivered hundreds of gender communication workshops and keynotes to numerous companies and trade associations across the country. This program consistently receives excellent reviews. It is successful for two reasons: people learn much more than they expect to, and they have more fun than they expect to.

The program is enlightening, light-hearted, educational, eye opening, and not male-bashing. This book follows this same approach and style. Keep reading!

## Here's What You Will Learn

1. You'll learn how stereotypes affect your perceptions of men and women, whether they use a predominantly masculine or feminine communication style.

2. We'll examine how your attitude about gender differences affects the productivity of your communication. Many women feel uncomfortable calling attention to their differences. They think that doing so will contribute to the salary gap and the glass ceiling and will cause men to resist women as peers and superiors. But denying who we are and ignoring our differences will only mire us forever in the puzzle of confusion.

The point is, *we are not the same – but we are equal.* Understanding and even celebrating our differences will help us learn to work together more effectively.

3. You'll learn about the biological and social differences between men and women and how they powerfully influence communication. We are built differently inside and out – it's no wonder we communicate differently! For example, a woman's lower brain is larger than a man's - this is where emotions and verbal capabilities are housed.
Women generally feel and show emotions more strongly than men, so men often think women are "too" emotional. In reality, women may appear to be more emotional because they have easier access to their feelings, actually feel many of them more strongly, and express them more readily, but that doesn't mean they are *too* emotional. Men may be more aggressive due to higher levels of testosterone, but that doesn't necessarily mean they are *too* aggressive.

4. We'll compare behavioral style differences. You'll see many general styles that men and women use. Some of them oppose each other, and this opposition leads to communication problems and

conflict...otherwise referred to as the puzzle.

5.    Then we will dig into specific communication differences and how they cause misunderstandings and misperceptions between the sexes. This is where all the preceding information comes together in a profound way. You will learn how you've been misperceiving people using the opposite sex style, and at the same time, how you may be being misperceived by others. Simply understanding these differences is half the battle. And, you'll also learn ways to handle specific and common communication conflicts.

For example, for hundreds of thousands of years men were responsible for hunting meat, building, protecting – saving lives, basically. For this reason and others addressed in this book, men generally tend to be more brief and solution-focused, and less detail-oriented, than women. For eons they didn't have time for details.

Most women are detail-oriented. They bond through talking and sharing. So when men don't offer details, women often perceive them as intentionally and rudely withholding information, pulling some kind of power play. Not necessarily. It's just a style difference. We'll discuss in depth many differences like this and the subsequent misunderstandings and conflicts they cause.

> *"Everyone is kneaded out of the same dough, but not baked in the same oven."*
> **Yiddish proverb**

## Of Course, There Are Exceptions

Generalizations are, by definition, not true of everyone in a group. There are unquestionably many cultural, geographical, and generational differences that affect the differences I discuss in this book. Two examples of cultural communication differences include these:.

Latin men naturally stand very close to those they talk with, much closer than most Caucasian American men feel comfortable with. Many Asian people, both men and women, do not use the same level of eye contact that most American women do.

Consider this book a good foundation of information, and know that you will see yourself and others using both masculine and feminine communication styles. And that's perfect. We all are a blend of both! Many of us don't realize it, though, and inadvertently run into conflicts and confusion because we don't understand how we are perceived by others. At the same time, we misperceive others whose styles differ from our own, making the puzzle pieces hard to fit together.

You may think you've heard all about this subject, but I promise you, you'll learn and be reminded of things in this book that will help improve your communication with both men and women. You'll become aware not only of the differences but why they exist and how to understand and work with them. In the workplace, this awareness and understanding leads to improved productivity, stronger teamwork, higher sales, more effective customer service, improved recruiting and retention results, increased confidence and job satisfaction, and reduced stress. At home, it leads to less conflict and more harmony and contentment. Let's get started.

*"If we cannot now end our differences, at least we can help make the world safe for diversity."*
**John F. Kennedy**

CHAPTER

# 1

# STEREOTYPES: ASSUMPTIONS AND JUDGMENTS

*"If you judge people, you have no time to love them."*
**Mother Theresa**

Every one of us, to a certain extent, believes some of the old gender stereotypes, especially if stereotypes are viewed as innocent descriptions of general behavior tendencies. Regardless of the significant progress in diversity issues being made throughout the workforce, stereotypes of some sort will always exist. The important thing to remember is that the simple presence of gender stereotypes is not the problem. Difficulties occur when stereotypes are used, however subconsciously, to prejudge people's abilities and competence and develop unfair and incorrect expectations. When that happens, effective communication, along with productive relationships, are jeopardized and thwarted.

When a staff member expresses frustration by crying in the office, do observers quietly doubt her competence on the job? When a management consultant interrupts his client several times during a phone call to discuss an upcoming project, is he automatically assumed to be quite rude and insensitive? If a new marketing manager brought homemade cookies to the office, would others question her management and decision-making skills? If an outspoken, driven, aggressive sales director mentioned he had two children, would some people wonder, at some level, if he were a gentle and loving father?

# Try This Exercise

The following simple yet meaningful exercise will help demonstrate the effect of seemingly innocent stereotypes on judgments of others. It will take only a few minutes, and there are no wrong answers. Very quickly, using your first impression, indicate beside each adjective below which sex the word best describes. Use "M" for Male, "F" for Female, and "B" for Both only if the word immediately brings to mind both men and women. Be honest and record your very first response.

| | | | |
|---|---|---|---|
| Entrepreneur | B | Emotional | F |
| Scuba diver | B | Competitive | M |
| Critical | M | Football fan | M |
| Hiker | B | Courageous | B |
| Funny | F | Powerful | B |
| Cheerful | F | Impatient | M |
| Likes children | F | Too sensitive | F |
| Lifeguard | B | Hates spiders | F |
| Intelligent | B | Competent | B |
| Good cook | F | Daring | M |
| Romantic | F | Gentle | F |
| Fussy | F | Warm | F |
| Horseback rider | B | Likes flowers | F |
| Skydiver | B | Self-starter | B |
| Impetuous | M | Dynamic | B |
| Persistent | B | Loving | F |
| Assertive | M | Fashionable | F |
| Intense | M | Independent | F |
| Nurturing | F | Daring | M |
| Committed | B | Competent | B |
| Talkative | F | Outspoken | M |
| Logical | B | Compassionate | F |
| Intuitive | F | Driven | B |
| Creative | F | Intelligent | B |

Glancing over your responses, notice the number of M's, F's, and B's. Most people get a good mix of all three. Looking at the list of adjectives, is there any one word that could not describe either sex? If not, then all the M's and F's you recorded indicate subtle and subconscious (and sometimes not so subconscious) stereotypical beliefs. Everyone has them...myself included.

Keep in mind that simply believing that some of these descriptions are gender-based is not wrong, nor a "bad" thing to do. Stereotypes, particularly those related to gender, often develop from observed behavioral generalities.

----

### Problems occur when stereotypes are used, however subconsciously, to prejudge people's abilities and competence and develop unfair and incorrect expectations.

----

For example, probably close to 100% of those completing this exercise indicated Female for the descriptions of emotional and nurturing and Male for the words aggressive and competitive. Speaking in general terms, are women usually more emotional than men, at least from what others can see? Of course. Are men usually more outwardly competitive than women? Yes. Again, the stereotypes in of themselves, or in a vacuum, are not the problem.

However, if stereotypes are used to form opinions about other elements of a person's capabilities or behavior, then problems arise. Doing so is not only unfair...it is judgmental and assumptive.

*"Assumptions allow the best of life to pass you by."*
**John Sales**

Reviewing the list again, could it be describing one person in different situations? Could that person be either a man or a woman? Most people agree that, yes, the list could be describing a man or a woman. Actually, the list describes me, as viewed by my friends and business associates. Of course there were many more adjectives than those included here (and of course, I selected mostly good ones to list in the exercise!).

Just for fun, take the test again. This time, however, use yourself as the person you are scoring. Check the adjectives you think best describe you most of the time, no M's or F's or B's necessary, only checkmarks by the words you feel apply to you in most situations.

**Descriptive Adjectives – Which apply to you?**

| Entrepreneur | ✓ | Competent | ✓ | Intense | ___ |
| Emotional | ✓ | Good cook | ___ | Independent | ✓ |
| Scuba diver | ___ | Daring | ___ | Nurturing | ✓ |
| Competitive | ✓ | Romantic | ✓ | Daring | ___ |
| Critical | ✓ | Gentle | ✓ | Committed | ✓ |
| Football fan | ___ | Fussy | ✓ | Competent | ✓ |
| Hiker | ___ | Warm | ✓ | Talkative | ✓ |
| Courageous | ___ | Horseback rider | ___ | Outspoken | ✓ |
| Funny | ✓ | Likes flowers | ___ | Logical | ✓ |
| Powerful | ___ | Skydiver | ___ | Compassionate | ✓ |
| Cheerful | ✓ | Self-starter | ✓ | Intuitive | ✓ |
| Impatient | ___ | Impetuous | ___ | Driven | ✓ |
| Likes children | ___ | Dynamic | ✓ | Creative | ✓ |
| Too sensitive | ___ | Persistent | ✓ | Intelligent | ✓ |
| Lifeguard | ___ | Loving | ✓ | | |
| Hates spiders | ___ | Assertive | ✓ | | |
| Intelligent | ✓ | Fashionable | ___ | | |

## What's The Point?

Notice how many adjectives you checked that generally apply to your gender. We apply stereotypes to ourselves too! The key point demonstrated by this exercise is this: just because a woman may be emotional, "too" sensitive (meaning more sensitive than the person judging her behavior) in certain situations, nurturing, and a good cook, does not preclude her from also being decisive, competent, intelligent, and driven.

Just because a man might be decisive, intense, logical, and independent does not mean that he is not also nurturing, sensitive, gentle in certain situations, and a good cook.

An employee may express emotion differently than her manager does, and that's fine. Her emotion does not necessarily translate to poor management abilities. The sales director certainly seems like a focused, driven, aggressive man. But chances are that he turns those hard-charging sales qualities off when he goes home to be with his children.

Bottom line, differences in style do not necessarily mean differences in skill.

## Stereotypes Are Just That

Stereotypes are neither reliable job performance indicators nor accurate descriptors of someone's complete personality. During communication, before responding to another's "stereotypical" behavior or comments, evaluate the clues available. Searching for the whole picture will enhance communication and result in a more objective, meaningful, and productive outcome.

*"Better keep yourself clean and bright; you are the window through which you must see the world."*

**George Bernard Shaw**

CHAPTER

2

# BIOLOGICAL DIFFERENCES

*"If the world were a logical place, men would ride side-saddle."*
**Rita Mae Brown**

Consider the biological differences between men and women...they're numerous! When you think about it, doesn't it make sense that if we are built differently, inside and outside, physically and genetically, that we would be wired to communicate differently?

The scientific and medical communities are just now discovering that every physiological system in the human body varies between men and women. Every single one. The same treatment for the same disease will yield different results in men than in women.

In December of 2004, abcnews.com published an article entitled "How Gender-Specific Medicine Could Change Health Care – Researchers Say Doctors Must Consider Gender Differences When Treating Women." In this article, Dr. Marianne Legato, chairwoman of the Partnership for Gender-Specific Medicine at Columbia University, wryly offered, "Women are more than just boobs and tubes. In fact, we are different in every organ system of the body, including the brain, the heart, the gut – even our skin is different from that of men in important ways."

On cbsnews.com in March 2005, Dr. Leonard Sax, a psychologist and family practitioner, said, "Girls and boys differ profoundly in how they hear, how they see, how they respond to stress – and those differences are present at birth.

In April 2006, the headline of an article written by Ronald Kotulak, a science writer for the Chicago Tribune, read this way: "Gender and the Brain – New evidence shows how hormones wire the minds of men and women to see the world differently." In the article, Larry Cahill, a neurobiologist at the University of California in Irvine, says, "The bias of mainstream neuroscience for the last 25 years has been, 'OK, sure there's some sex differences way down deep in the brain in this little structure called the hypothalamus, but otherwise the brains of men and women were pretty much the same. That was wrong, as wrong as could be."

Scientists thought that sex differences were generally controlled by the hypothalamus, a small organ in the brain. Recently, however, a hormone called kisspeptin has been discovered, which at puberty triggers other hormones, which in turn stimulate estrogen and testosterone, initiating physical changes. Blocking kisspeptin prevents these changes from taking place. This hormone bath also affects the brain and impacts female/male characteristics. And this is just one difference.

Another intriguing recent finding was published in the journal Nature in the fall of 2005. That study identifies the genetic difference between men and women at about 1 percent. Comparatively, the genetic makeup of chimpanzees and humans differs by only 1.5 percent. So, women and men differ genetically almost as much as humans differ from chimpanzees! Huntington Willard, a geneticist at Duke University and coauthor of the Nature article said, "You could say that there are two human genomes, one for men and one for women."

Entire books have been written about biological differences between men and women. My objective in briefly discussing merely a few biological differences in this book is to underscore their prominence and impact on communication.

# MEN

- Fewer nerve endings

- Thicker skin

- More body hair

- Better daytime vision

- Larger lungs

- Thicker skull

- 10% taller

- 40% muscle, 15% fat

- 50% stronger arms, stronger thumbs

- Spatial talents develop at average age 6, earlier than in females

- Better at math and science in early years (gap diminishing but still present)

- Better at thinking three-dimensionally

- Emotions controlled in amygdala with no direct connection to language or reasoning center

- Brain 9% larger than women, but with same number of brain cells

- Ten to 100 times more testosterone than women

- Larger portion of brain (2.5x) more devoted to sexual pursuit

- Larger portion of brain devoted to action and aggression

- More serotonin = less depression

- Men notice subtle signs of sadness in a face 40% of the time, women - 90%.

# WOMEN

- Less body hair
- Better nighttime vision
- Sweat glands more evenly distributed
- Joints more flexible
- 23% muscle; 25% fat
- Evenly distributed fat layer
- Better oxygen supply to the brain
- Female babies less fretful, smile more, eat less, control bladder earlier
- Up to 40% more connectors in brain; larger corpus callosum
- Spatial talents develop at 13, later in life than males
- Larger area of brain devoted to emotion and memory.
- Stress shuts down sex drive more quickly
- Emotions controlled in cerebral cortex, along with language and reasoning
- Generally 15% more blood flow to areas of brain for emotions and memory
- At least when young, 2-4 times better hearing than boys
- Advanced cell growth in verbal hemisphere at age four; better at reading and writing early in life although men score higher on college exams
- Talking for connection stimulates dopamine and oxytoxin, significant neurological treats.
- Women use about 20,000 words a day; men - 7,000
- More lung cancer and gallstones
- Less pancreatic cancer

(Sources include: Male and Female Realities by Joe Tannenbaum, and The Female Brain by Louann Brizendine, MD)

Hundreds of thousands of years ago, in the time of the caveman (I use this period because it comprises the largest piece of our evolution relevant to the beings we are today), men were primarily responsible for hunting meat, building shelter, and protecting tribe members. Saving lives, very simply put. The biological differences listed above support and reinforce those responsibilities. If men were out in the elements, hunting and building in inclement weather, they needed more protection. Thus, fewer nerve endings, thicker skin, and more body hair.

As hunters they needed to be able to see enemies coming, and to spot, chase and kill game. Therefore, better daytime vision was necessary and larger lungs were required to allow more oxygen into their systems. All temptation to tease put aside for the moment, the thicker skull feature probably made men more likely to survive if they received a blow to the head. (From a frying pan, several women in my workshops have suggested with a smile.)

Men are taller, they have more muscle than fat, and they have stronger arms and thumbs. Equipment suited for building and protecting.

> Doesn't it make sense that if we are built
> differently, inside and outside, that we would
> be wired to communicate differently?

Men, at young ages, are generally better at math and science. (Can't believe I have the nerve to speak this truth, given the reaction to Lawrence Summer's inappropriate yet not so incorrect comments.) There are more male math prodigies. Men's brains are organized a bit differently than women's, and they have a small advantage with math, science, and logic at birth. This difference is also encouraged by the fact that generally, more boys are interested in math and science than girls.

Yes, this heightened interest is due in part to teachers gently guiding boys that way as a result of their own programming and interests. This gap is narrowing significantly as time goes by, however. Women need only to be interested and apply themselves to compete equally in math and science. Education can, has, and continues to eliminate this general small difference in scientific aptitude.

Same with three-dimensional thinking. This difference has helped men with building, working with spaces and shapes, and with spatial relationships like figuring out the distance and trajectory when they're throwing a spear or using a slingshot. Reading maps and having a good sense of direction flows from this spatial-thinking difference too.

Research has shown that men find their way using measurement, logic, and physics – women more often use landmarks. Case in point – Mary, a friend of mine, is a top executive with a large healthcare organization. She is highly intelligent, assertive, and a good manager. When I called to get directions to her home, where she has lived over nine years, she handed the phone to her husband to help me.

Keep in mind once again, though, that these interpretations are generalities and can easily be impacted by exposure and education. The growing number of excellent women architects, scientists, astronauts, and physicists attests to this fact.

On a lighter note, there are also some modern day reasons that these differences exist. Better daytime vision...so they can find their golf ball in the rough! Stronger thumbs...helps explain their vast superiority with the remote control, don't you think? (Don't worry men, I joke about women too. We must laugh at ourselves and our differences, after all, *they are funny*. Let's not take ourselves too seriously!)

*"It is of immense importance that we laugh at ourselves."*
**Katherine Mansfield**

# Biology And Communication?

What do these biological differences have to do with communication? Quite a bit, actually. These differences are deeply ingrained. They are part of our wiring, our programming, and they are not going to fade away.

Men are built to be physically stronger than women – they had to be more physically powerful in order to fulfill their responsibilities. In the past, before language was developed and refined, men, much more often than now, used brute strength to get what they wanted. They are used to simply pushing their way through, so they come across as more direct, aggressive and insensitive.

Still today they feel innately responsible for women's well-being and survival. That's why it disturbs so many men when women cry. They feel like they've failed, let down the woman, reinforcing one of their deepest fears – not being needed and appreciated. At some level, however unconsciously, they think the woman is deeply troubled or in trouble and they must save her. For all practical purposes, for men tears = impending death. That's one reason why men often fire off solutions instead of just listening. They feel honor-bound to fix everything.

*"Just as the difference in height between males is no longer a realistic issue, now that lawsuits have substituted for hand-to-hand encounters, so is the difference in strength between men and women no longer worth elaboration in cultural institutions."*

**Margaret Mead**

Men are more left-brain oriented, using logic and reasoning more so than relationship and verbal skills. Overall, these physical differences exist because of hormonal differences, most specifically testosterone, and hormones rule everything.

In an article "Why Do Men Act The Way They Do?" by Andrew Sullivan, reprinted from the New York Times Magazine by Reader's Digest in September 2000, Sullivan calls synthetic testosterone a "metaphor for manhood."

"Men and women differ biologically mainly because men produce some 10 times as much testosterone as most women do, and because this chemical profoundly affects physique, behavior, and mood." Sullivan reports that testosterone's effects start early. Men experience a flood of this hormone three times: in the uterus a few weeks after conception, during the first few months after birth, and again at puberty. (Many experts now claim that men have 10-100 times more testosterone than women.)

When researchers injected newborn female rats with testosterone, they went on to develop male mounting behavior. Newborn male rats that had the hormone blocked failed to develop normal penises, and presented themselves to untreated male rats in a way typical of female sexual behavior. In our society, males commit more crimes, 4 to 1, than females, and the proportion is even higher with violent crimes. Blue-collar workers have more testosterone than white-collar workers, according to a study of more than 4,000 former military personnel.

Sullivan, the author, takes injections of synthetic testosterone, and has no desire to quit – even though it is attributed to increased male aggression, baldness, heart disease, and prostate cancer in black men. Sullivan claims that the hormone gives him more energy, appetite, and strength. His advice? "Let's use our increasing knowledge of the "He" hormone to understand what it is to be a man, for better and for worse. Let's accept how men and women aren't created equal – and move on." After substituting the words "the same" for "equal", and encouraging a similar knowledge increase of the "she" hormones, I agree.

Other results of the male fetal testosterone wash - women have 400% more neurons then men in the brain centers for language and hearing; men have 2.5X brain space devoted to sex, as well as larger centers for action and aggression. In women, the control center for anger and aggression is larger, not the center itself, so it's generally easier to anger a man.

By the way, an important aspect of biological differences, actually any differences, involves those *among* women and *among* men.

Sometimes these differences seem greater than those between men and women. Why? First, because there are notable differences between people. Second, we expect familiarity and sameness, to a degree, with people of the same sex as ourselves. When they don't fit the mold, or our expectations, the differences seem exaggerated and more apparent. And, of most impact, there are significant genetic differences among women and again among men.

Reviewing female biological differences, women's primary responsibilities hundreds of thousands of years ago included pregnancy, childbirth and rearing children. The biological differences you see above help support those responsibilities. More flexible joints, less body hair, more evenly distributed sweat glands, a higher level of fat than muscle especially as compared to men, better oxygen supply to the brain... all these physiological differences support pregnancy and childbirth.

In addition, research made public in November of 1998 at a meeting of the Society for Neuroscience in Los Angeles, indicated that motherhood may make women smarter – perhaps permanently – as hormones released during pregnancy and nursing dramatically enrich parts of the brain involved in learning and memory. As new mothers, intelligence and resourcefulness would be very valuable for the sake of children's health and survival.

A larger corpus callosum, which is the connective tissue between the right and left hemispheres of the brain, and a larger portion of the brain dealing with emotions, are thought by some researchers to give women a leg up on relationship-building and communication skills. Of course, just as women can compete successfully in math and science, men can improve their skills in these verbal/intuitive areas with study and practice.

Emotions being controlled in the cerebral cortex also helps explain why women generally feel and express emotion more readily, more visually and more verbally, than men. Physiologically, men cannot access their feelings and emotions as easily as women can. The difference in visible expression of emotion is one of the biggest trouble spots or puzzle pieces between men and women.

Physiologically, men cannot access their feelings
and emotions as easily as women can.

USA Today reported in July 2002 that a study conducted by a team of psychologists using brain scans discovered that women's brains are better organized to perceive and remember emotions. "The wiring of emotional experience and the coding of that experience into memory is much more tightly integrated in women than in men," said Turhan Canli, assistant professor of psychology at State University of New York – Stony Brook, the lead author of the study.

These findings support the "myths" that women remember arguments longer, hold grudges, and are more susceptible to clinical depression, as dwelling on and reviewing memories is a risk factor in depression.

Women were (and generally still are, to a large extent, although increasing numbers of men are getting more involved with their children every day, to everyone's benefit) responsible for raising children. It takes not only nurturing relationships and communication to do that, but also attention to detail, intuition, and more connection with emotion. That larger corpus callosum, the connective tissue, allows for more whole-brain thinking, integration of both the right and left sides of the brain.

Brain areas responsible for emotions, memory and tracking gut feelings are larger and more sensitive in women. Who knew? Biology explains women's intuition. Most emotions in men trigger rational thought, not so much gut sensation.

Pain areas in women's brains are visibly activated when they see or are told that other people are in pain. Men's brains do not respond the same way.

Spatial talents develop in girls later in life than in boys, however this difference may eventually narrow as girls get more involved in sports at early ages. But we're talking evolution here, so any changes in the brain won't happen overnight.

As far as modern reasons for these differences... a few women in my workshops suggest that they learn how to control their bladder earlier in life so that later, they can last longer shopping without having to stop. (Yes, women and shopping is a stereotype. And it's true. In general, women like to shop MUCH more so than men do. And there's nothing wrong with that, just like there's nothing wrong with the fact that more men like to hunt and build things.)

Those are merely a few of the biological differences between men and women. Even our brains set us up for communication conflict and confusion, and in a big way. Then menopaused hormone variations come into play, changine a considerable amount of what I just wrote. I strongly recommend the book *The Female Brain* by Louann Brizendine, MD.

I must give voice to those authors and experts who disagree with the theory that gender brain differences lead to behavioral, performance, or personality differences. Actually, some people even disagree that male and female brains differ. I subscribe to the theory that anyone can find research to support just about any belief they may hold. Personally, I find the information outlined in this chapter to make good sense; it helps me to understand some of the obvious general behavioral variations between men and women. Many experts and scientists agree. Some don't. My suggestion is that you absorb what feels right to you and put aside the rest for later digestion and consideration.

CHAPTER

# 3

# SOCIAL DIFFERENCES

*"Society is one vast conspiracy for carving one into the kind of statue it likes, and then placing it in the most convenient niche it has."*
**Randolph Bourne**

Communication between men and women is further confused by social conditioning. Throughout the centuries, gender-based responsibilities helped program us with characteristics necessary to adequately handle such duties. These are certainly generalities, and some coincide with the biological differences discussed in Chapter 2, but they exist nonetheless. Unfortunately, they also predispose us to the negative impact of stereotypes as well, as explained in Chapter 1.

These social roles, along with child-rearing, strongly contribute to the glass-ceiling phenomenon. The Simmons School of Management, a business school designed specifically for women, founded the Center for Gender and Organizations and has conducted several studies regarding gender dynamics in the workplace.

One recent study of 471 senior-level women showed that women with children were less likely to leave their jobs and more likely to be satisfied with their advancement opportunities. This finding flies in the face of the belief that senior women are opting out of the workforce due to family responsibilities.

The fact is, most women who do leave re-enter the workforce within a year, either with new jobs or self-employed. A shallow look at the numbers often leads companies to believe that women have less commitment to work, therefore those organizations invest less in developing women as leaders. The issue is that women who left didn't want to work for that specific company, for a variety of reasons depending on each woman's particular situation.

A second dynamic assumes women don't want to be leaders or aren't willing to do what it takes, to make the necessary sacrifices to get ahead. However, another study by the Center for Gender and Organizations of 226 senior managers at a professional services firm found that equal percentages of men and women aspired to the corner office. Even so, compared to 67 percent of the men, only 47 percent of the women had been offered leadership development opportunities. Executives assumed women didn't want development and weren't offered it.

A third study of 570 professional women indicated that 72 percent wanted to be influential leaders in their companies and 47 percent wanted the top job.

## Gender-Based Social Attributes

## MEN

- Strength, aggressiveness
- Competition and superiority
- Independence
- Hiding and denying emotions
- Brief and focused

## WOMEN

- Strong desire for monogamous relationships
- Consensus, harmony, conflict avoidance
- Attention to detail; fine motor skills
- Strong verbal and social skills
- Highly developed intuitive and people-reading skills

If men were responsible for hunting, building and protecting, doesn't it make sense that they were programmed for strength, aggressiveness, competition and superiority more so than women? This programming was for survival, a matter of life or death. To keep himself, his family, and his species alive and protected from harsh weather, enemies, and predatory animals, a man needed to feel superior and be competitive. He had to stand up to threats and danger from predators of all kinds, human included. He also needed these characteristics for dominance, control and victory over other tribes to ensure the growth and longevity of his own group.

If he went on month-long hunting or "manhood" treks, independence would be very important, wouldn't it? If he stood in front of an enemy and burst into tears, that wouldn't bode him very well - he would likely be killed on the spot. Hiding or denying emotions became a way of life, literally one tool to stay alive. And men were responsible for saving lives – keeping the species alive and growing - so they were brief and focused. They didn't have time for details.

---

**To keep himself, his family, and the species alive, a man needed to feel superior and be competitive.**

---

Due to other survival issues and responsibilities, women were wired differently. As much as women hate to admit it now, back then, they needed men's protection to survive (Ayla in *Clan of the Cave Bear* and other superwomen notwithstanding). If an enemy or a saber-toothed tiger killed a man, or if another woman stole him away to replace her previous partner, his female partner and her children would likely die.

These situations also explain some of the innate, subconscious competition between women today. Social programming is deep and enduring, also in many cases subconscious. This survival instinct is centuries and centuries old, it is solid and it is ingrained. Women are programmed for monogamous relationships much more so than men because it meant life or death to them.

......................................................................................................

As much as women hate to admit it now, back then, the protection by men was critical for survival. During that time in evolution, women HAD to have men to stay alive.

......................................................................................................

A monogamous relationship to men meant fewer offspring, and threatened survival of the species. Men were programmed to procreate and keep the species alive, to strengthen their tribes through sheer numbers. As I tell my audiences in a humorous tone, "Gentlemen, this is no longer necessary. There are plenty of human beings on the planet now!" This tendency is best adapted to fit current social norms. So, we have deeply ingrained gender-based differences in life-and-death, survival issues, resulting in a totally contradictory approach to relationships. And we wonder why there's conflict and confusion between men and women?

*"Men always want to be a woman's first love –*
*women like to be a man's last romance."*
**Oscar Wilde**

Because women's responsibilities included raising children, women are wired to a greater degree for consensus, harmony and avoiding conflict. Also, a woman didn't want to make her man angry because if he left, she might die. Raising children and gathering fine seeds and grains gave women more of an attention to detail. (In one of my programs for a corporate client, I had just made this comment about attention to detail and fine motor skills, then waved my arm while talking and knocked a glass of water all over my materials. A decidedly male voice in the back called out, "So much for fine motor skills!")

Strong verbal and social skills, and highly developed intuitive and people reading skills manifested in women due to their responsibilities for relationships and child rearing. In fact, many experts give woman more credit than man for the survival of the species due to woman's singular involvement in raising and caring for children, and consistent gathering of non-meat food.

These differences can be observed in children today: boys play cops and robbers, cowboys and Indians. Girls play dolls and house. Early play teaches boys competition, leadership, and hierarchies, while girls learn relationships and conflict avoidance. Young boys will gravitate toward the cars and trucks, and girls toward dolls and tea sets, regardless of parental influence. Nature magazine reported in early 2006 that even baby monkeys demonstrate the same toy preferences.

Pat Heim, who holds a doctorate in communication and has written several books on the topic of gender communication, has observed that men offer friendliness, whereas women offer friendship. A subtle, yet profound difference. "Friendliness comes and goes as needed to get something done. Friendship is a relationship that overrides the project," she said. Heim attributes this difference to childhood practices. Men grew up playing on teams with boys they didn't necessarily like, and learned to pull together anyway. Women grew up with more choice and control over who they socialized with, so liking someone became crucial to their ability to create a relationship. One result of this socialization is that men are more goal-oriented, and women are relationship- or process-oriented.

In practice, both skills are needed for project management success, another reinforcement that men and women are suited to work well together – it just takes commitment to understanding and working with our differences.

# CHILDHOOD SOCIAL MESSAGES

It's important to acknowledge childhood social messages. Your first response might be that people don't reinforce these messages in their children anymore, that society is much more enlightened now. It's not that simple. Once again, ingrained programming doesn't die quickly or quietly. Every single one of these messages will be familiar to you, which means they are still seeping down the generational ladder. Yes, things are changing, but the saying "Boys will be boys" was penned for a reason and it will stay.

I teach this information, and even though I do not repeat these messages per se, I still find myself treating my nephews in a more rough-and-tumble way than I do my nieces. The truth is, being male, they *are* more rough-and-tumble, as are most boys (but not all…again, there are exceptions to every rule). Any one who disagrees with that comment most likely has not spent much time with children of both genders. Even so, my behavior with them reinforces some of the typical gender differences – men more aggressive, women more gentle and sensitive, etc.

Is that so bad? Frankly I don't think so. I have no desire to see the two sexes blend together and become alike. None whatsoever. I do not, however, tell my nephews not to cry or my nieces to be nice and sweet. And playing more gently with little girls is by no means communicating to them that they are any less intelligent or less capable of great success or in any way unequal to boys. Generally speaking, they aren't as physically strong, which in no way hampers their ability to be fulfilled, contributing, successful people. Below are some common social messages reinforced throughout many a childhood:

## For boys...

- "Big boys don't cry." This message does not help men learn how to be sensitive and express emotion.

- "Be the man of the house. Be tough." Again, no indication of sensitivity and emotional support or expression. Also, socially, men are not allowed to be vulnerable, as such behavior from the male gender is perceived as weak.

In her article "Say Cheese" in the Los Angeles Times in April, 2000, Ellen Alperstein discussed a study conducted by David Dodd, a psychology professor at Washington University in St. Louis. Dodd studied yearbook photos of students from elementary school through college, comparing smile rates. Up until fourth grade, he found similar smile rates. By fourth grade, 89% of girls smiled compared with 77% of boys. By ninth grade, the gap grew to 70% versus 43%.

The study didn't set out to cover old information, that girls smile more because they are socialized to please. Dodd wanted to identify when the difference became significant. He determined that the gap manifests when kids become interested in the opposite sex. By the end of elementary school, Dodd said, children are receiving messages to behave differently, relative to sex roles and the ideals for the different genders. The ideal girl for boys is pleasant, humorous, nonthreatening, and carefree. The ideal boy for girls is strong, silent, athletic, serious, Dodd reports.

Once again, boys need to be tough and strong to meet social norms.

## For girls...

- "Sit there, be quiet and look pretty." This teaches a girl to bury her opinions, and to be indirect and unassertive. Worse yet, it communicates that her greatest feature and characteristic is her appearance, not her values, ethics, intelligence, or personality. This wiring wreaks havoc on self-esteem and leads to eating disorders, depression, lack of self-awareness, obsession on appearance and wardrobe, etc.

- "Be nice and sweet if you want to get a husband." Forget sharing your other admirable qualities, like your brain and power. This also reinforces men's fear of being manipulated by women.

  (During a program I did recently for a high-tech sales group, I was writing this last message on a flipchart, and as I wrote, ...if you want to get a _____," I heard a female voice in the back call out "lower quota!")

- "Don't hurt anyone's feelings." Right. Hold it all in. Don't say anything, don't cause conflict. This philosophy has caused widespread repression of feelings and therefore significant income for therapists. I'm not advocating being rude or offensive, but I do support standing up for yourself and being honest, in a compassionate and responsible way.

Regarding the first point above, society's pressure and emphasis on women's appearance have not improved much. Barbara Brotman of the Chicago Tribune wrote an article shortly after the Enron scandal broke titled "When A Woman Blows the Whistle." Brotman quotes Stephen Kohn, board chairman of the National Whistleblower Center, "What motivates a whistle-blower is gender-neutral." However, Kohn said that gender differences arise in how a female whistleblower is treated.

"You're going to face retaliation, some form of professional or personal insult whether you are a male or female," he said. "But if you're a female, there's a strong chance they will look at your appearance and your sex life, and use that as a basis to insult you or issue derogatory statements. That will not happen with a male."

Kohn said that's what happened to Linda Tripp, former Pentagon assistant who secretly taped her conversations with Monica Lewinsky. Tripp's appearance was ridiculed significantly by the press, so much so that she underwent extensive plastic surgery once the hoopla quieted down. Of course, the circumstances of this whistle blowing differed greatly from those involving Sherron Watkins of Enron, who wrote a letter to her CEO to warn him of impending doom. The key difference between the two was an issue of loyalty – Tripp betrayed her friend for questionable (at least to the public) reasons while Watkins was viewed as trying to help her company. Whatever the motivation, the attention on Tripp's appearance was sad and unfortunate.

---

The key to successful communication is to be aware
of our differences and understand how to work with them.

---

## We ARE Different!

As you can see, men and women are VERY different, and that's good! We are different from the moment of conception, and those differences are reinforced socially. It's nature AND nurture combined. Think how boring life would be if we were all the same. We would be like R2D2 or C3P0 robots running around, all looking the same and acting the same. No thank you! I love it that men are different than I am. We should celebrate that we are different.

The key to successful communication is to be aware of our differences and understand how to work with them effectively. Recognize the subtle stereotypes you may carry, and be very careful not to make assumptions or judgments from them. Again, being more emotional doesn't necessarily translate to weak or indecisive management skills. And being more aggressive and driven doesn't exclude one from being a gentle loving partner and parent.

*"And woman should stand beside man as the comrade of his soul, not the servant of his body."*

**Charlotte Perkins Gimman**

CHAPTER

4

# BEHAVIORAL STYLE DIFFERENCES

*"Sometimes I wonder if men and women suit each other. Perhaps they should live next door and just visit now and then."*
**Katharine Hepburn**

The biological and social differences discussed in previous chapters translate to behavioral style differences between men and women. Reasons for confusion and conflict will become even more apparent as you see how these styles aren't just different, they basically oppose each other. You'll see yourself in this information, and you'll recognize people you work with and people you love.

## LEARNED OR INBORN BEHAVIORS

| MASCULINE | FEMININE |
|---|---|
| • Independence | • Consensus |
| • Superiority | • Inferiority; equality at best |
| • Status | • Connection |
| • Competition | • Harmony |
| • Be respected, admired | • Be liked, approved of |
| • Withdraw under stress | • Talk under stress |
| • Bond through talks & activities | • Bond through feelings & problems |
| • Allowed: anger and aggression | • Allowed: tears, fear, confusion, tenderness |
| • Not allowed: tears, fear, tenderness | • Not allowed: anger, confusion, aggression |
| • Difficult to ask for help | • Don't mind asking for help |
| • Handle conflict directly | • Avoid, fear conflict |
| • Speak briefly and to the point | • Discuss things in detail |

Let me say right away and again that these behavioral styles are generalities. There are always exceptions to the rule...I am a perfect example. I find myself on both sides of the list, depending on the circumstances. In many business situations, I can be direct and assertive. I will engage in conflict if I feel mistreated or taken advantage of, even though while doing so I often feel tentative and frightened inside. And I can be very conscious of my time, so when I'm busy at work I am quite brief and focused and avoid lengthy discussions unless they are absolutely necessary. I am known by my friends as a direct communicator and a sensitive, loving woman.

But we must start somewhere, and these generalities provide a foundation to work with. That's why I label them as "masculine" and "feminine" styles rather than "male" and "female" – all people have a combination of both styles. Understanding these differences, whether with a woman using a masculine style, a man with a feminine style, a woman with a feminine style, etc., will help you improve the productivity and effectiveness of your communication.

---

### These behavioral styles are generalities... there are always exceptions to the rule.

---

## Independence vs. Consensus

Starting at the top of the list, men were largely programmed for independence and superiority (due to past duties of hunting, protecting, battle, etc.). On the other hand, responsible for relationships and considered less important (due to less obvious role in survival and to help position male dominance), women were programmed more for consensus and inferiority. At best, even today, equality.

Consider the dinner rituals of my family. When I was a child, with six siblings, dinner together was the norm. Dad and Mom sat at opposite ends, with the kids lining each side of the table. Mom brought

Dad the serving dishes, he served himself then passed the food on to the kids and Mom. Did I care that I didn't get served first? Absolutely not. But the underlying, subconscious message sent was that men are more important. At dessert time, Dad got a clean fork while the rest of us licked the food off our dinner forks and reused them. Again, the message that men are more important than children and women. Society is becoming more savvy, but this programming has been part of our make-up for hundreds of thousands of years and it's not going to go away anytime soon.

As will be addressed in Chapter 6, men don't apologize nearly as often as women do. Superiority programming leads to this characteristic. One example involved a female attorney friend of mine who reports to a male. Before leaving on a business trip, Barb asked her boss to call a client for her and determine her authority level ($ damages) for the mediation scheduled the day she returned. This is common practice; there was nothing unusual with this request.

The day of the mediation, Barb was down to the wire, the mediation was to start in less than an hour, and she hadn't heard from her boss yet as he was late arriving at their office. Finally he appeared, skirted all around the subject of the authority level, and left her to make decisions with no client consultation or approval. He had forgotten to call the client, never admitted it, and never apologized for his oversight. Barb told me that the next day he avoided her like the plague. Guilt rearing its ugly head. Did Barb confront him with the truth? No. She may be an attorney who excels in litigation, but she still hates conflict and confrontation. (This feminine characteristic is discussed later in this chapter and in Chapter 6.)

Another manifestation of the lone-wolf nature of men is evident in their definition of responsibility. Author Anne Wilson Schaef, in her book *Women's Reality* (HarperSanFrancisco, 1992), explains that men think of responsibility as accountability. When something goes wrong, the responsible person gets blamed. Women tend to see the person responsible as the one who can and will respond when something needs to be done. Blame is rarely involved.

## Competition and Status vs. Connection and Harmony

Again because of leadership and protection responsibilities, men are wired more for status and competition than women, whereas women are wired more for connection and harmony. The status-connection difference is profound and permeates most interactions between and among men and women.

Even in conversation these differences are demonstrated. According to Deborah Tannen, Ph.D., expert on gender communication issues and author of *You Just Don't Understand: Women and Men In Conversation* (William Morrow, 1990), men often view conversations as "negotiations" in which they try to achieve status and maintain independence. Very often this competitive approach is a conscious tactic. Women, on the other hand, tend to see conversation as a way to connect with other people.

I'll share a story from my good friend Fred. It illustrates the competitive nature of men, both with other men and with themselves.

On a blistering hot afternoon in Washington, DC, Fred was attending a party after work, in a courtyard outside a downtown bar. He was on his way out when he spotted an attractive woman ("a babe" in his exact words) in the corner. He thought he should at least try to talk to her or he'd be thinking about her all night. As he worked his way through the crowd toward her, he told himself, "I'd better say something clever, something that will sweep her off her feet, something that will set me apart from all the other dudes on the prowl."

.................................................................................................................

The status-connection difference is profound
and permeates most interactions between
and among men and women.

.................................................................................................................

Suddenly, Fred was face to face with her, and what came out of his mouth was, "So, is it, is it, hot enough for you?" Lame line, he admits, but they started talking, and two years later, Fred and Ellen were married.

Some time later, Fred asked his wife, "Darling, what did you think? What came to mind when I approached you that day in the courtyard?" She responded, "Well, you were wearing a yellow shirt, and that made you look sallow (Ellen is an image consultant), but I did think you might be a warm guy."

Fred wasn't clear on what all that meant, so he opened the dictionary. The definition for sallow was "almost dead." Ugh, he thought. But he was feeling pretty good about "warm" until he found the definition for that word..."not so hot."

Fred's competition with himself and perceptibly all other single men in Washington for the attention of an attractive female was successful in the long run, but according to him, in no way due to his wit or the first impression he made. A note of caution to men, however – don't try so hard. Women are often put off by super-smooth lines and what appears to be practiced flirting and pick-up behavior. A little nervousness is appealing to many women because they interpret the man as really wanting to make an impact. ("Maybe he likes me so much it makes him tongue-tied.")

Another friend of mine, Bill, was a flight attendant in the mid- to late 70's, when men had just begun entering into that field. Bill encountered the competitive nature of men several times, from pilots. He said many of them were quite territorial and coveted being the only men on staff. The pilots viewed heterosexual male flight attendants as competition for attention from female flight attendants.

In one situation, one of Bill's male colleagues delivered a pilot's meal to the cockpit. The pilot actually told him to take it back and have a female flight attendant deliver it! I was happy to hear from Bill that the flight attendant put the tray down in the cockpit, told the pilot that was his meal and he could eat it if he wanted to, and then went on with his work in the passenger cabin.

# Respect vs. Like

Men prefer to be respected and admired; women prefer to be liked and approved of. Be very clear that I am not saying women don't want to be respected and admired, or men don't want to be liked. These are generalities and preferences.

Many women, including myself when first in the business world, are in denial about this difference and several others. I told myself, "I don't care if they like me or not, I need to be respected to get ahead!" Yes, I did need to be respected to get ahead, but the truth is I also wanted to be liked, and still do. I simply wasn't being honest with myself because I felt it sounded weak and lightweight. If I had to choose between the two, in most business situations I would select respect, but overall I would prefer both. Because of men's more independent nature and superiority programming, along with sports teams experience since childhood, they can more easily compromise on the "like" aspect and strive for respect.

# Stress – Withdraw vs. Talk

Men tend to withdraw under stress. Remember, they were programmed for independence and superiority, and think they should solve their own problems, alone. If you have read *Men Are From Mars, Women Are From Venus* (which I recommend), you may recall that John Gray tells us that men go into their caves when stressed. They don't want help; they want to figure it out themselves. So they go off some place where they can ponder the issue alone and process it.

On the opposite end of the spectrum, women talk under stress for two reasons: they bond through sharing feelings and problems, and they are more verbal. Talking through issues helps them process and understand. A very different style. What happens? Men see and hear women talking about all these problems and think, "Good grief, she's going to have a nervous breakdown any second now!" No, it's just a style difference.

Women experience men not sharing problems or discussing feelings and take it personally. As you can see, this style usually has nothing to do with anyone else, it's just the man's preferred way of dealing with stress. He needs his down (cave) time, his decompression hour, as I've heard it referred to.

## Bonding Styles

Men bond through tasks and activities – working on the car, playing sports, painting the house, building a garage. As I just mentioned, women bond primarily through talking. When a woman's partner comes in from a game of golf and she asks him how the game was, what does he say? "Fine." Then she asks what he and his friends talked about. "Nothing." He's serious! And if they did talk about something at any length, he doesn't remember any details, good grief that was two hours ago. Even so, he feels just as close to his friends as she does to hers; it's just a different style of bonding. Neither of these styles is right or wrong, good or bad. Just different.

*"Women like to sit down with trouble as if it were knitting."*
**Ellen Glasgow**

Of course men do talk, but generally not to the degree women do and it's often about sports, hobbies, business, or other non-personal topics. And these differences are international. My friend Andrew in Sydney, Australia told me about the Great Aussie Barby Syndrome. This is where all the men stand around the barbeque talking about sports, and all the women sit somewhere nearby talking about kids or other "womanly" topics. Heaven help anyone who attempts a border crossing: Andrew advised that this is seen as treachery to your gender.

It has been determined by researchers that management tends to view male employees as task-oriented and female employees as people-oriented. This perception further supports the difference in bonding styles. However, these two orientations don't necessarily oppose each other, but compliment one another (as do many of the differing styles discussed in this book). Women report that if their staff is happy (as a result of her being people-oriented), they will work more productively and effectively (be more task-oriented). Deborah Tannen in You Just Don't Understand quotes a female manager, "If my people are happy, they are going to do a better job for me."

## Anger vs. Tears

It is socially more acceptable for men to show anger and aggression, whereas it is not socially acceptable for women to show anger and aggression. Yes, we are getting more open-minded and less judgmental about this, but we still have a long way to go. I've heard it said that in the workplace, when a man loses his temper and yells, it's viewed as taking control. When a woman loses her temper and yells, it's viewed as losing control. Think about it. Same behavior, totally disparate perceptions due solely to gender differences.

When a man loses his temper and yells, it's viewed as taking control. When a woman loses her temper and yells, it's viewed as losing control.

Hundreds of years ago, when the Japanese first started training the Samurai Warriors, they trained women as well as men. And women were just as accurate with their weapons as men. But they had to stop including women because they were being killed much more often. Why? Women would hold back and attack only when they were 100% certain that the enemy meant them harm. They couldn't be 100% certain until the sword was already in their bellies.

A woman in one of my workshops lamented the fact that her co-workers, both men and women, resented her for being more assertive and outspoken in meetings. This stems from both genders expecting women to be soft and harmonious. There is absolutely nothing wrong with women being assertive. My advice is to be polite and respectful at the same time.

Take opportunities outside of meetings to let your softer side show through...everyone has a softer side, by the way. As long as you truly treat others with respect and compassion, do the best job you can at work, and communicate clearly and politely with even emotion, you can't lose. Be yourself and sooner rather than later, others will understand and grow comfortable with your style.

## Asking For Help

It can be difficult for men to ask for help because of the status, independence, and superiority wiring. Of course, the first example that my seminar attendees mention is...asking for directions. (That's probably why Jimmy Hoffa is still missing – he refuses to ask for directions.) On the other hand, women usually don't mind asking for help. They'll pull over every two blocks if they have to. They make friends that way...and find new people to talk to.

> *"Today, if you are not confused,*
> *you are just not thinking clearly."*
> **U. Peter**

However, let's compare how men and women give directions. Usually when you receive directions from a man, you know exactly where you're going: south on Broadway, east on Main two blocks, second house on the right, number 4020. On the other hand, women are more visual, and detail-oriented. "You know where that little white church is on Main, down on the end? Yes, all the way at the end, that little cute church. Well, don't go that far."

A woman once directed me by phone, "Before you get there, you're going to *feel* like you want to go right, but go left instead." Interestingly enough, I trusted her. I thought, "OK, I'll come to a place where I'll want to turn right but I'm not supposed to. I guess I'll just know it when I get there." And I did.

And thus an example of the differences among women – with my more masculine style for giving directions, I would have described that turn in this way, "When you come to the fork in the road, take the smaller road to the left."

## Conflict – Direct vs. Avoidance

Men tend to handle conflict directly, again due to the status, competition, and superiority programming. Women, however, often avoid and fear conflict. They have been taught not to hurt anybody's feelings. They have been programmed that if they make someone mad, they might die. This is deep, deep stuff. In many cases women (especially some businesswomen) will engage in conflict, but only when they see no other alternative. This topic is addressed in further detail in Chapter 6.

## Brief vs. Detailed

Men, wired to communicate in order to keep people alive and to keep the species going, generally speak briefly and to the point. They communicate to solve problems, to figure things out, whereas women often communicate to bond, relate, and be understood. Combine that purpose with a larger portion of the brain devoted to verbal capacities and a socially wired attention to specifics, and you get women discussing things in more detail.

One of my sisters, Kathy, was the Assistant Administrator of a rehabilitation hospital in San Antonio. A patient turned in a complaint about one of the nurses that worked for Kathy, so Kathy asked the nurse to follow protocol by filling out a two-page report. Kathy sent it up to her boss, and it came back down in inter-office mail the next day with a note that said, "What does this say?" Kathy wrote on it, "Nurse did bad, nurse told if she does bad again she's fired." She sent it back up and didn't hear another word from her boss. That's all he wanted to know. He wanted the bottom line, and didn't want to read a two-page report. Style differences.

A business associate of mine is president of a high profile trade organization. One of the women who report to him, an attorney, keeps him posted, with excruciating detail, about every situation she is involved with. Her level of exactness is tiresome to many of her co-workers.

My friend is patient with her and allows her to work within her comfort range, which means making sure he knows everything that she knows, because she ultimately does very good work. He says it takes more time than necessary but he finds it a worthwhile investment, as the end product is very good. I think this attorney should count her blessings that she has such an understanding boss. Most men, and women with a masculine communication style, would not have the patience to listen to all the details regarding her legal forays and accomplishments.

*"The problem is not that there are problems. The problem is expecting otherwise and thinking that having problems is a problem."*
**Theodore Rubin**

Do you see how behavioral style differences can cause problems? We view the other sex through our own styles, and doing so often backfires. We judge and make assumptions that others are intentionally trying to be difficult, or withholding information, or being *too* emotional rather than simply *more* emotional. Putting it simply, we are programmed differently for survival reasons. Communication, and thus personal and professional relationships, are directly affected.

We view the opposite sex through our own styles, and doing so often backfires.

The next two chapters deal with communication specifics. These differences, and the misunderstandings they yield, are familiar, eye opening, and enlightening.

*"We first make our habits, and then our habits make us."*
**John Dryden**

CHAPTER

# 5

# COMMUNICATION PERCEPTION DIFFERENCES: MEN'S OR MASCULINE STYLE

*"If God wanted women to understand men,*
*football would never have been created."*
**Seen on a bumper sticker**

So very many communication problems stem from misunderstandings and misperceptions. We view others through our own lenses and experiences, and make judgments based on what we are used to and familiar with. We make assumptions, often inaccurately, from innocent style differences.

As you read through this information, I suggest that you view it from two perspectives. (1) How you might be *misperceiving* the opposite sex and (2) how you might be *being misperceived* by the opposite sex. It's important not only to adapt your perceptions *of* others, but also your behavior *toward* others. Why? Because it's going to take both men and women working together to stop this "battle between the sexes" and improve our communication and relationships.

........................................................................................................

It's important not only to adapt your perceptions *of* others, but also your behavior *toward* others.

........................................................................................................

Also, as mentioned several times in this book, please be aware that there are always exceptions to the rule. You will see yourself and others you know on both sides of the page, depending on the situation and people involved. For example, in business dealings for the most part I have a direct, masculine communication style. Why? I think because I have been in business for so long, working primarily with men for many years, and have learned the importance of focus, brevity and time management.

In my personal life, generally I have a feminine communication style…much softer and less assertive. That said, when I am in charge or responsible, whether a business or personal situation, my communication takes on a more direct tone. Not necessarily rude, just more to-the-point, assertive, and matter-of-fact.

I know women who are very direct and assertive in all arenas of life, and men who are indirect and soft in their communication. There will be exceptions, but again, we have to start somewhere as a foundation. To more easily comprehend and relate to these differences, consider the styles as masculine and feminine rather than male and female.

Notice the masculine styles listed below, and how women often misperceive and misunderstand men due to judging styles based on their own communication approaches and experiences. Men get labeled as jerks, power freaks, or other derogatory names, most often undeservedly. Women perceive them from a female perspective and judge them negatively because they do not behave in the ways women are most familiar and comfortable with.

> *"Knowing is not enough; we must apply.*
> *Willing is not enough; we must do."*
> **Johann von Goethe**

| MEN'S / MASCULINE STYLE | WOMEN'S / FEMININE PERCEPTIONS |
| --- | --- |
| Discuss problems infrequently | Aloof, tough, unfeeling |
| Talk to fix and solve problems | Men see women as weak and powerless and incapable of problems |
| Brief, focused, few details | Withholding information, impolite |
| Don't give same emotional support | They don't care |
| Listen silently; process internally | They don't listen or don't care |
| Avoid constant direct eye contact | They don't listen; avoid connection |
| Use aggressive humor and put-downs | Insensitive, mean-spirited |
| Take up more physical space | Controlling, higher status, more power |
| Make decisions independently | Don't value women's opinions |
| "Do this," "Give me this" | Demanding, bossy |
| "Girl," "Honey," "Gal," etc. | Don't respect women; feel diminished |

## Less Discussion of Problems

Due to their programming for independence and superiority, men discuss problems infrequently. Women, who often bond by discussing problems, even when they often know exactly what they want to do, view men as being tough and that nothing bothers them. Or, that men are just too aloof to talk about it. This is just another style difference.

In my workshops I conduct an exercise that involves the participants anonymously writing down something they wish the opposite sex understood better about them. In every workshop, in one way or another, at least one man writes that he wishes women knew how sensitive he is. Men may not discuss problems or express emotions as easily or frequently as women, but that doesn't mean they don't think about troublesome issues or feel them.

## GENDERSMART CLUE:

**Women, don't jump to conclusions that men are unfeeling and aloof. They just deal with their problems and feelings differently than you do. Men, recognize how women may perceive you and try to share some issues with those close to you more often, when appropriate. And know that it's appropriate much more often than you might think, particularly in your personal life.**

## Talking to Fix

Men talk to fix and solve problems. They were responsible for saving lives. This tendency runs deep - to solve problems whether help is asked for or not. I have this tendency as well. I've been in business for over 25 years, so I often assume when someone brings me a problem I need to fix it. I start firing out solutions. But that person may not want solutions. She or he just might want to share and process. So when men or people with this particular masculine style offer solutions, some women think, "Wow, he thinks I can't even solve my own problems and that I'm an idiot, incapable of dealing with this successfully on my own. That's not true, I'm just talking and sharing! I know what I need to do. It just helps me to process out loud."

Obviously, exceptions to the rule exist, especially in the workplace. If a meeting has been scheduled to address a problem, or someone actually states that they would like your opinion, then solutions are certainly called for. To optimize any communication, just tune in and pay attention. Better yet, if you are not sure of their objectives, ask if they would like ideas or if they prefer that you just listen.

## GENDERSMART CLUE:

**Do you see the difference and how the misperception happens? How do you avoid this intrusion? When someone brings you a problem, in your own words simply ask, "Do you want me to just listen, or would you like some ideas?" Then, the person discussing the problem needs to be honest about whether or not they want help or just a listening ear. So, just ask, and avoid the problem before it occurs.**

## Brief and Focused Approach

Men are very brief and focused, offering few details. Superiority and independence programming yields this behavior. (Many engineers, architects, and scientists would be exceptions to this particular style, at least in the workplace. Shower them with details about the neighbors or a soap opera, however, and they just might fade away and tune out like many other men in any industry.) As a result of different styles involving level of detail, women sometimes see men as intentionally withholding information and consciously pulling a power play.

A man walks out of a meeting. A female co-worker walks up and asks how the meeting went. He responds, "Fine." She asks what was discussed. He says, "Oh, the usual stuff," and walks on down the hall. She is left standing in his dust, incredulous that he so blatantly ignored her request for information and bonding and purposely kept important information from her.

A misperception, in the vast majority of cases. Chances are that by the time he got 10 feet down the hall, he already forgot she even asked about the meeting. He simply is not predisposed to detail and once the meeting was over, shifted his focus to the next life to save.

## GenderSmart Clue:

If she (or whomever asked for more information) needs more detail for a report, or just plain because, all she needs to do is ask more specific questions. "Hey John, what's the latest on the Wilson project? What did Melissa say about the new directives?"

Men, please understand that detail to women is like...beer, cars, sports or steak to you. It's nourishment! (I am aware I am stereotyping here, in a gentle, humorous way. This comment in no way jeopardizes the status of men. We must take ourselves less seriously in order to achieve harmony.)

## Less Emotional Support

Men don't tend to give the same level of emotional support that women do. They have been trained not to show feelings, so women think, "Wow, he's not comforting me or saying anything sweet or putting his arm around me...he just doesn't understand me or care about me!" Not necessarily so. Many men show their feelings through tasks, by taking care of the family financially, keeping the yard trimmed and mowed, running errands, fixing the broken cabinet. This sounds like 1950's rhetoric, but it is still applicable today in many cases.

*"Love builds bridges where there are none."*
**R.H. Delaney**

Take sales, for example, as an area where this lack of outward emotional support becomes apparent. In a survey conducted in 1997 by Judith Tingley, author of *GenderFlex: Men and Women Speak Each Other's Language At Work*, both sexes reported that the male salesperson's greatest perceived weakness was lack of genuineness and honesty.

In a November 1998 Forbes magazine article, Jim McCann, President of 1-800-FLOWERS, said, "When guys sign a big deal, we don't run out of the office screaming 'yeeeah!' Women are quicker to do that. So when I want to announce good news around here, I make sure that the group includes women. They tend to be demonstrative, and that makes the whole room feel better. It's good for morale."

One way in which men show emotional caring and support for each other is through physical contact, or roughhousing. Bodychecks, shoulder punches, fake boxing, for example. Most women find these activities unpleasant. As a child, my older brother would often ambush me from around a corner and punch me in the arm or pinch-twist my skin. I understand now this was his way of bonding with me and expressing his affection for me, but it drove me crazy at the time. Actually it would drive me crazy now too.

In a gift book entitled Live and Learn and Pass It On, by H. Jackson Brown, Jr., a 19-year old contributor wrote, "I've learned that when coming home from college, if your little brother wrestles you to the ground, it's his way of telling you he loves you."

> ## GenderSmart Clue:
>
> This is mainly a style difference, a programming gap that can be bridged with a little awareness and effort. Men, know that most women expect and need more emotional support than you are used to giving. Women, don't assume that men don't care. They just may not show it as readily and obviously as you do. Tell them what you need, as specifically as you can, and remind them politely, yet directly, from time to time. Be aware that most women must get 60-70% of their emotional needs met by other women!

## Silent Listening

Men tend to listen silently. They process things internally, and again, they aren't supposed to show feelings and emotional responses – doing so makes them feel weak and vulnerable. You can pour your heart out and sometimes you're lucky if you get a blink. Generally, women are just the opposite, eyes in full contact with great expression, arms flying about like a floppy scarecrow in shifting winds. "Oh my gosh! You've got to be kidding! That's so terrible, wait 'till I tell Marsha!" Tremendous activity going on - you know the woman is listening. It's just a style difference.

*"A good listener tries to understand thoroughly what the other person is saying. In the end he may disagree sharply, but before he disagrees, he wants to know exactly what it is he is disagreeing with."*
**Kenneth Wells, in Guide To Good Leadership**

A small study conducted by the Indiana University School of Medicine in 2000 revealed in souped-up MRI testing that while listening, most men showed activity only on half their brain, the left side. Most women showed activity on both sides. Interpretation? Several. Women want to give their full attention, it's part of bonding and relationship orientation. Men often listen out of need, not desire, so they are not fully engaged. Women listen with both logic and emotion. One possible conclusion could be that women have to work twice as hard to listen. However, most studies indicate that few people would agree with this interpretation.

Both men and women rate women as better listeners, but this is not always the case. Because women are programmed to create harmony and consensus, they are more inclined to put something aside in order to listen. But remember how I said men are more brief and focused? If a man is focused on a game on TV, or on reading the newspaper, he won't hear you. The same goes for me when I'm reading a book. Someone has to tap me on the shoulder to get my attention if I'm truly engrossed in what I'm reading.

Another manifestation of the "men don't listen" complaint was explained to me by an audience member. He teaches skiing lessons to children. His experience has been that the girls stand still, listen carefully, and learn faster than the boys. The boys, on the other hand, are running around, raising havoc, distracting him and the girls, and therefore are not as skilled as the girls when the lesson ends. They may have had more fun though.

> *"We have two ears and one mouth so that we can listen*
> *twice as much as we speak."*
> **Epictetus**

Interruption styles vary significantly also. Men speak without pausing, feeling free to interrupt each other to take turns. Women often speak with intentional pausing, allowing others to take turns. Interruption is used for urgent additions only. As a result, women see men as controlling and intentionally shutting out women's contributions, and men view women as timid and their interruptions as pushy and too emotional.

Conversational styles are influenced by other factors in addition to gender. Culture, religion, ethnicity, geography, and upbringing, to name several. Gender differences are just one way to help make sense of style differences, a good way in my opinion because we all can readily identify men from women and we all can relate to this obvious variation between people. Looking at differences from a gender perspective is sometimes criticized as oversimplified, but if that's what people can understand and relate to, if it makes sense to them and is not inaccurate, what's the harm in being simple?

## GENDERSMART CLUE:

My advice is twofold: Women, be strategic and selective about the times you choose to discuss something important with a man, and realize he will not give you the level of obvious listening clues you are most comfortable with. And men, dial up your active listening skills. Keep in mind how you are being perceived by people trying to communicate with you.

## Less Eye Contact

In the past, and still to some degree today, it was a sign of aggression for men to hold direct and constant eye contact. Men also often think that if a woman holds steady eye contact with them, she is flirting. Consequently, men avoid lingering eye contact, which causes women to assume that men are not listening and are avoiding connection.

*"People only see what they are prepared to see."*
**Ralph Waldo Emerson**

Deborah Tannen conducted a study that involved this listening issue. Tannen filmed three sets of girls and three sets of boys, ages 5, 10, and 15. She put each set in a room with two chairs. In every case regardless of age, the girls sat so they could maintain eye contact. They either positioned the chairs facing each other, or turned their bodies on their chairs to accommodate eye contact. In every case, again regardless of age, the boys sat side by side, shoulder to shoulder, looking around the room, at the carpet, or picking their nails, avoiding eye contact.

Dr. Tannen also filmed adults in organizations across the country. The same behavior was documented. Women would crane their necks during meetings to see around co-workers in order to establish eye contact with the person speaking. Men would stare ahead or play with their pen or paper, both while speaking and while listening.

I use relatively direct eye contact when communicating with women or men. When speaking with a man, I tune in and watch his eyes and body language. Every once in a while, I can tell when a man starts to wonder where I'm coming from. I can see in his face if he starts to wonder whether I'm flirting. If I see that clue, I avert my eyes for a second or two to break the connection momentarily.

As I mentioned, there are always exceptions to the rule. One male executive whom I met with recently, for all practical purposes, stared me down during our entire meeting. In over 20 years in business I had not encountered this level of direct eye contact. He never broke his gaze, never wavered, hardly blinked. Was this flirting? No, it was aggressive, power-positioning, controlling behavior. I conducted my presentation as usual, held his gaze, and ignored the bait.

On the other end of the spectrum of power-based eye contact (or lack thereof) is a situation previously experienced by a client and good friend of mine, Kris. A few years ago Kris planned, coordinated, and staged a national convention for the company she worked with at the time. A major undertaking, as any meeting planner knows.

Toward the end of the planning stage, the president of the company decided to get involved, and wanted to cut back on the number of attendees, most of whom had already been invited. Kris and her boss sat in the president's office as he read the list of attendees and questioned each one. Kris patiently explained the rationale for each person. Not even once did the president establish eye contact with her. He looked at her boss, a male, as he asked questions and then either again at her boss or at the list in his hand as Kris answered.

In my opinion this goes far beyond gender differences and poor eye contact, this is poor management. Even though she knew this executive had a reputation for this kind of distasteful behavior toward women, Kris felt her presence was ignored and that she was treated rudely, and I agree with her. I think, in addition to gender differences, part of the president's behavior might have been due to the fact that he didn't know Kris' name, but that's no excuse to ignore someone. And if that was the case, considering this was Kris' first meeting with the president, her boss should have made introductions when they first entered his office. (Read another aspect of this same meeting in the apologies section in Chapter 6.)

---

## GenderSmart Clue:

As you have probably guessed by now, I advise women to acknowledge and understand that many men will not maintain the steady eye contact women feel most comfortable with. This does not mean he is not listening or connecting with you. If it distracts you a great deal, touch his arm to attract his attention (if appropriate), or tell him in your own words that you prefer eye contact to best concentrate and ask gently for his cooperation in doing so. Men, I suggest trying to increase your direct eye contact, especially with women who expect it from those they speak with.

# Aggressive Humor

Men tend to use a more aggressive style of humor, one in which they put others down. Women, coming from harmony programming, find this style offensive, and because they don't laugh when men do this, men think women don't have a sense of humor.

> *"A difference in taste in jokes is a great strain on the affections."*
> **George Elliot**

Subconsciously, this aggressive humor behavior comes from a place of attempted superiority, as putting someone down has the subconscious objective of boosting the "put-downer" into a higher, stronger, more superior position. They put others down to raise themselves into a perceived higher position. It's the status thing.

In *You Just Don't Understand*, Deborah Tannen refers to this as "one-up" behavior. Men's behavior supports their world in which they are either one-up or one-down. Their intra-gender approach to humor involves intentionally offending each other, consciously and/or unconsciously establishing dominance and hierarchy. In most cases, men are not intentionally trying to be offensive, this style is their way of doing business, so to speak. It's all they know, it's the hierarchy they were socially wired for and raised in.

Anne Wilson Schaeff, in *Women's Reality*, expands on this concept by explaining that when two people come together, men automatically assume that one of them must be superior and the other inferior. There's no in-between. Often, men do not necessarily want to be one-up, but given the only other choice of being one-down, they will compete for what they see as the superior position.

Perhaps this helps explain many men's difficulty with the concept of equality.

Boys always have leaders, coaches, bosses, and people above them in rank. Hierarchy is a way of life for them. In *Smashing The Glass Ceiling*, author Pat Heim points out that girls are raised in more of a flat hierarchy where no one is "boss." If a girl tries to take over as leader she is ostracized from the group. With more and more girls involved in sports, however, females are being exposed to the hierarchical approach.

Women rarely use a one-up style of aggressive humor, being wired to maintain harmony and not hurt anyone's feelings. Therefore, women often interpret men as being insensitive and mean-spirited, and men view women as not having a sense of humor.

## GENDERSMART CLUE:

Neither perception is true. Once again, style differences lead to assumptions and misunderstandings. And women do have a sense of humor, of course. It's just a different kind of humor.

Both sexes would benefit from keeping and displaying a healthy, non-aggressive sense of humor. Many people, both men and women, are successful with this approach. Laughing together, with each other, not at each other, demonstrates acceptance and respect.

## Space = Power

Men generally take up more physical space. They cross ankle over knee, put feet up on desks, spread papers out in meetings, and drape their arm over the back of the chair next to them. Space conveys a subtle message of power. Women, smaller and softer and more physically contained ("Sit there, be quiet, and look pretty." "It's not feminine to sit like that!" Not to mention it's not appropriate with a dress or skirt on.), are perceived as less powerful, confident, and effective.

## GENDERSMART CLUE:

Women, spread your papers out, put your arm on the chair next to you...take up more space!

## Independent Decisions

Due primarily to status, independence and superiority wiring, men tend to make decisions independently. They process things internally. They "don't want to talk about it." They don't ask others for their opinions as often as women do. As a result, women think men don't care what they think, that men don't value women's opinions. "He doesn't think I have anything to offer because he's not asking what I think." This independent style also often sends the message that men are aloof, avoiding connection, and poor team players vying for power and control. Again using an opposite style, women often approach decisions with a consensus style, asking others for their opinions even when they know what needs to be done. This is discussed more thoroughly in the next chapter.

## GENDERSMART CLUE:

Women, avoid jumping to negative conclusions and recognize this style difference is most likely contributing to your discomfort. Men, try using a participative style and ask others what their thoughts are. Not only will you help them feel valued and respected, you just might get some keen insight and good ideas.

## "Do This!"

To many women, men seem to fire out orders. A noticeable lack of "please" and "thank you" tends to make men's requests and instructions come out as harsh, demanding, and bossy. Women feel they are rudely told what to do without warmth or caring. On the other hand, these same women, in an unconscious effort to maintain harmony, say please and thank you a little too much.

Craig Rydin, President of Godiva Chocolatier, said in "Surviving in

No-Man's-Land," an article in the November 1998 edition of Forbes, "If you are a command-and-control type of manager, forget about working for a company with a lot of women." Whether Mr. Rydin meant it or not, his comment applies to command-and-control men and women. Especially women who supervise other women. Due to the flat hierarchy I mentioned previously, women expect members of their own sex to treat them as equals, not subordinates. Many women have a great deal of trouble taking orders from other women, even more so than from men, due to this equality expectation.

---

## GENDERSMART CLUE:

**We can use some balance here. Men could give a few more pleases and thank you's. Women could use a few less as too many can draw power from their statements, and therefore from how their capabilities and confidence are perceived.**

---

## Patronizing Remarks

Any group that has been oppressed for a long time, and is just now pushing its nose above the waters of equality, is going to feel disrespected and put down when referred to with terms that are not equal. "Man/woman" are equal. "Man/gal" are not. "Man/honey" are not.

I am of the opinion that over 95% of men who use these terms do not intend to be offensive. It's a habit, it's an endearment, it's a better choice than "hey you!" when they can't remember her name. I think a tiny minority of men do use these terms as a power play, but so few they hardly deserve attention in this particular book.

In a past career as Senior Vice President of Sales and Account Service, I was in a meeting with a boss who called me "honey" in front of an important prospect. That prospect was not yet familiar with my capabilities, so my boss' comment concerned me a great deal. I felt minimized and feared the prospect would not take me seriously.

Interestingly, my boss and I were good friends and he was one of my biggest fans. He knew the value of my work and expertise. I knew at the time he meant it as an endearment, but my concerns were well founded. And I explained all this to him after the meeting.

Otherwise, such terms rarely offend me. I try to focus on intention. But that is my approach and may not work for many women who may have experienced other forms of belittlement or disrespect.

If these terms bother you, that is understandable and perfectly acceptable. You have every right to your feelings. My reaction to these words is my personal reaction only. The key is, if they do offend you, you must say something, directly and with warmth.

> *"If we don't change, we don't grow.*
> *If we don't grow, we aren't really living."*
> **Gail Sheehy**

In some cases, a man may be trying too hard to be cool, to connect with women. Example: I was facilitating a mastermind group of female financial services producers in their branch office. One of the managers stuck his head in the door and asked with a smile, "What's going on in here, a Tupperware party?" His question was answered with a stony silence, and he retreated. The women didn't ignore him, they were truly shocked into silence by his thoughtless remark. Many women would say he was intentionally trying to demean them. In some cases that may be true, but in this instance, knowing him, I believe he was literally ignorant about how to connect with and respect women. I honestly think his intentions were pure, but the results were negative.

Actually, these days I hear more of the "gal, honey, and sweetie" terms from women than I do from men. I use such endearments for my friends and family. My best friend calls me Janie Baby, a couple friends call me Honey Bunny. Rather than being offended, I am touched by their expression of caring, which is their intention. Purely innocent. Over the past few years, men have been beat over the head, and rightly so in some cases, about sexual harassment and related issues, so often they are more hesitant than women in this arena.

Here's the way I look at it. Thank God for feminists because they helped women get where they are today. But in order to get from where we were to where we are, feminists had to go way out on the equality/feminist scale. Where we have settled is somewhere in between. In the meantime, while way out at the end of the feminist scale, many men and women were alienated, offended, and threatened, including myself during the early Eighties. I worked in a male-dominated environment and I was afraid the feminists would make men angry, making it tougher for me instead of better. I was focused on the short-term result instead of the long-term benefits.

Men got scared to death to open a door for a woman, or offer to help with luggage for example, for fear of getting their heads bitten off. "I can do it myself!" Those women were just trying to fight for independence and equality. Even so, by coming across stronger than men are used to seeing women, feminists pushed the genders apart for a while. A necessary separation, as pain often precedes healing and growth. Remember this phase of the women's movement?

I perceive things to be lightening up in the past few years. Chivalry is coming back. Because women have gained ground and respect, and men are a little more comfortable with women in the workplace, people seem to be relaxing a bit. For years no one would offer to help me with my luggage on a plane, and now men regularly offer to help me. I love it.

But chivalry may be a double-edged sword – is it based on men's perception of women as being weak? That's the negative view. Again, women generally are not as strong as men. So let's say men's perception of women is that of being more gentle, less physically strong, deserving of tender care and attention. That's the positive view. Besides, these days, most polite people hold the door for anyone coming behind them, man or woman.

Let's go back to the 95% rule for a moment. The majority of both men and women have the best intentions in mind. Perhaps up to a maximum of five percent of men use patronizing terms, or chivalry, as a power play to intentionally offend someone and put them down, and up to five percent of women overreact. They've been fighting for equality for so long I don't blame them for having a chip on their shoulder. But over-reaction will not solve the problem, it will only serve to inflame it.

........................................................................................................

## If these terms are not acceptable to you, you must say something!
## Be direct, with compassion and respect.

........................................................................................................

A couple years ago I was walking down the hall at a convention with a woman friend as two men were walking toward us. My friend and I were looking at each other (eye contact), and the men were watching the floor (avoiding eye contact). Neither pair was looking straight ahead. One of them slammed into my friend, almost knocking her over. He grabbed her by the shoulders to steady her and said "Oops, sorry babe!" She snapped back quite maliciously, "My name is Gail!" The man who bumped into her raised his eyebrows and put his hands protectively in front of him, "Whoa, okay, okay!" and then tiptoed, carefully with exaggeration, around us and on down the hall. I was embarrassed. A more appropriate response would have been "I prefer to be called Gail," or "Please, call me Gail!" in a friendly tone of voice.

To me, that chance bump in the hall didn't lend itself to correction, unless Gail knew she would see that man often, or if he had used such remarks with her before. But that's my reaction - pick your battles. Again, it is perfectly okay if these terms are not acceptable to you. But you must say something!

People can't read your mind and by letting the opportunity to speak up pass, you're basically giving him or her permission to keep using the offending behavior. Be direct, with compassion and respect. You don't have to blast them between the eyes. (Blasting is reserved for more serious offenses, such as sexual harassment or career-damaging behavior.) No one likes to be blasted, and few people respond positively to this aggressive kind of approach. You are trying to solve a problem, not exacerbate one. But again, if repeated warnings fall unheeded, or the behavior is serious, blasting may be appropriate.

## GENDERSMART CLUE:

The best course of action? Use genderless, nonsexist terms such as: everyone, everybody, people, managers, technicians, etc. Even "ladies" is a bit sensitive because of "Hey Lady" and Lady of the Evening, although that sensitivity is lessening as time goes by and women become more confident about their position in the workplace and in society. I am aware that many men think the term "ladies" is the refined and preferred label, but it's a double-edged sword. When approaching a group of women at the elevator, for example, "Hi women" sounds silly, "Hi ladies" is a little risky, so try "Hi everybody."

The term "guys" is becoming gender-neutral as well. I often use this term from time to time in my workshops once rapport has been established as I have a conscious desire to keep my communication informal and casual. With every style difference addressed in this book, remember there are also cultural, geographical, and age variations. Certainly I would stop calling people "guys" in a heartbeat if I thought I was offending anyone. No one has said anything, ever. My hope is that someone will speak up if "guys" does not work for them. One of my messages with this book is to encourage readers to lighten up and work together on these types of issues. Let's stop taking ourselves so seriously with these relatively minor infractions!

*"We cannot change anything until we accept it. Condemnation does not liberate, it oppresses."*

**Carl G. Jung**

CHAPTER

6

# COMMUNICATION PERCEPTION DIFFERENCES: WOMEN'S OR FEMININE STYLE

*"You can complain because roses have thorns, or you can rejoice because thorns have roses."*

**Ziggy**

Let's talk about women's communication styles and how men often misunderstand and misperceive women. Just as women do with men, men view women through their own lenses and perspective, and then judge accordingly. This often results in negative judgments and assumptions. Men, notice how you might be misperceiving people with a feminine style, and women, notice how men or those with a masculine communication style might be misperceiving you. Again, we need to adapt our perceptions and our behavior – it's a two-way street.

It is very interesting to note that these misperceptions of feminine style differences contribute substantially to the existence of the glass ceiling. This business phenomenon keeps women from being promoted to the highest levels in so many companies, and from advancing at the same speed as their male counterparts. Men, still comprising the top positions, often view female employees as weak, indecisive, vague, less credible, lacking confidence, and ineffective. Men misunderstand women's softer communication style, leading to these faulty judgments. So many don't promote women or mentor them to executive spots. This serious predicament is changing, but it has a long way to go.

In *Talking From 9 to 5*, Deborah Tannen points out that when corporate leadership changes or departments are reorganized, the remaining employees and managers jockey for position. When possible, they try to move in on positions held by women because they are perceived as being more vulnerable and less competitive.

Why? The men perceive women's communication and interpersonal style through their own lenses and experience of superiority, competition, one-up, etc. These lenses aren't wrong, they're just different and therefore a feminine style in the business arena is, in a way, foreign to men. These are merely style differences, not differences in intelligence, capability, confidence, or effectiveness.

| WOMEN'S / FEMININE STYLE | MEN'S / MASCULINE PERCEPTIONS |
|---|---|
| Discuss decisions, make by consensus | Indecisive, insecure, incompetent |
| "Let's do this", "How about this?" | Weak, not management material |
| Don't boast or sell | Insecure, underestimated themselves |
| Discuss problems and feelings | Too emotional, troubled, weak, hold men responsible for their problems |
| Handle conflict indirectly or avoid it | Less credible, weak, conflict unimportant |
| Handle conflict directly and firmly | Bossy, bitchy, harsh, witches |
| Nod and encourage speaker | Agree with everything men say, insincere |
| Use tag questions, apologies, disclaimers | Less credible, indecisive, vague, no power |
| Make indirect requests | Covert, sneaky, manipulative, ineffective |
| Cry and express emotion more often | Weak, too emotional, manipulative |

## Decisions by Consensus

Women, being very consensus-oriented, often discuss decisions. They may know exactly what they want to do, but because they want people to feel valued and involved, they ask others for their opinions.

Men, who generally make decisions independently, see women asking for input (for help, in their view), and assume women can't make their own decisions. Men see asking questions as a losing proposition, as an activity that makes them appear incompetent and less effective. One-down. If they ask questions, they must be inferior, unintelligent or not savvy about what's going on. Therefore, men conclude that women are indecisive, insecure, and thus not good management material. Hello, glass ceiling.

*"The doors we open and close each day decide the lives we live."*
**Flora Whittlemore**

Yielding what seems to be opposing information, a seminal study conducted by Robert Kabacoff, Ph.D., Director of Research at Management Research Group, compared 900 female and 900 male managers. This study indicated that while men delegate more and are more inclined to cooperate with colleagues, female managers are perceived as more assertive and competitive in achieving their goals, maintaining more control of their projects.

The operative word in that last sentence is "perceived." Both men and women are not used to seeing women in assertive roles, so playing that card comes across much more strongly. In other words, both men and women notice assertive behavior by women more so than they do men, because they expect men, not women, to be assertive. Consequently, truly similar behavior by men and women is perceived and judged differently. My guess would be that the managers, male and female, had very similar beahvior but the women were judged more harshly.

In addition, many women have fought so hard for their positions and careers that they often continue the fight when it is no longer necessary. Or, they dial up their assertiveness too high, at the expense of good interpersonal skills. They fear being seen as incompetent, and therefore feel they have to do everything themselves, as forcefully as possible, to prove their value and ability. As you can imagine, and probably have witnessed, this over-assertive behavior will only backfire at some point, either personally or professionally.

## GENDERSMART CLUE:

It would seem self-defeating to suggest that women stop asking others for their opinions. Women can, however, learn to power-up their requests for input. "I have a solution in mind that I think may work, but I'd sure like to have your input." Also, women can power-up other elements of their communication to help offset the misperceptions caused by their inclusive style.

And very importantly, men, please understand this simple style difference and avoid making assumptions about women's competency based on their softer styles of communication and management. It would be ideal, of course, if both sexes recognized the value of participatory management, delegation, polite and compassionate leadership, and teamwork.

## Inclusive Language

Another way this softer style of communication plays out is with inclusive language. For example, when giving directives or assignments, women often say, "Let's do this, okay?" or "How about if we do it this way?" What they intend and are thinking is the masculine version: "Do this," or "Here's what I want you to do." But they don't want to be viewed as harsh or bossy (remember they have been programmed not to be direct or hurt anyone's feelings) so they soften communication, positioning orders as requests or suggestions.

Also, according to Deborah Tannin in *Talking From 9 to 5*, female managers often intentionally downplay their authority with male employees so as not to threaten them. Women use softer, inclusive language and consensus to accomplish this effort. "Here's the problem. What do you think we should do?" Instead of, "Fix this problem please."

Men, who use a stronger, more direct style, witness this softer approach and again assume that women are weak and incompetent, too indecisive for management positions. It's just a style difference. Just as often as men, women know what needs to be done, they just don't want to feel like they're cramming it down anybody's throat.

And that brings up another aspect of these style differences. Being more direct with instructions and assignments, unless you are rude or literally bark out orders, would not be viewed as cramming anything down anybody's throat. The relationship and harmony programming in women is so deep even they view their own direct communication as too harsh, when most often it is not. Being direct and also compassionate at the same time will reduce misunderstandings of your requests, and also misperceptions of your management abilities.

## GENDERSMART CLUE:

"I'd like the report done this way, please." Direct, clear, strong, and polite. Also clear but not quite as strong is "Let's do it this way" – inclusive, yet still unmistakable due to avoidance of phrasing the directive as a question. On the other hand, "How about we do it this way?" lacks confidence and power.

## Selling Yourself

When young, girls are taught not to brag by both their parents and playmates. Mothers will say, "Oh, don't say that, you sound like you're getting a big head! Remember, be nice and sweet." And playmates will ostracize boastful girls because they expect equality, fairness, and an even playing field, an equal hierarchy, from each other. Girls learn not to brag or talk about their accomplishments and strengths because they will lose their friends. Even as adults, women often downplay their strengths and advantages so as not to alienate other women. Loss of friendships or acceptance can be very traumatic to the gender that revolves around relationships.

Consequently, girls who don't brag grow up to be women who don't sell or promote themselves within organizations and don't publicize their accomplishments. Unlike men, who, according to Deborah Tannen in *Talking From 9 to 5,* understand the importance of displaying the behavior associated with the next job up the ladder, women tend to feel it would be presumptuous to act as if they had power they don't yet have. As a result, men (or women comparing employees of both sexes) underestimate female staff and see them as insecure.

> *"What we say and what we do ultimately comes back to us so let us own our responsibility, place it in our own hands and carry it with dignity and strength."*
> **Gloria Anzaldua, in Words In Our Pockets**

In an interview for the Washingtonian magazine in November 1997, Tannen recalls a situation where a female boss suggested to her direct report, a male team leader, that a female team member be promoted into a position a male team leader was looking to fill. He said, "She doesn't want to be promoted." His boss suggested that he ask her. He did, and to his surprise, she wanted it. Yet she obviously had never communicated, at least not clearly and directly, her ambition or desire to her team leader.

During a workshop I conducted for a major Fortune 500 client on Authentic Leadership for Women, the highest ranking woman in attendance, a Senior Vice President, remarked after an activity addressing career development, "It never occurred to me to just ask for what I want." Amazing.

In this same article mentioned above, Tannen explains that a journalist who once interviewed her commented that he noticed this dynamic when comparing coaching styles of boys and girls. Unconsciously assuming the girl athletes would behave the same as the boys, he watched for the best girl athlete, figuring she would be the team leader and tell all the other girls what to do. But he couldn't easily identify who was best from their behavior toward each other like he could with the boys. He had to watch them play, because the girls who were best acted like the others and didn't flaunt their athletic superiority or throw their weight around off the field.

This also explains, at least partly, why women in high positions often have more problems with other women than with men. Executive-level women have learned the hierarchy game and how to promote themselves. Lower-level women are still holding onto the flat-hierarchy socialization of childhood, where all girls are "equal." In actuality they never were equal, but the higher status girls learned quickly not to spotlight their position. So, when a woman behaves like a male boss and claims her power and position, some women complain and feel betrayal and resentment. When a male boss does the same thing, his behavior isn't an issue.

Speak with confidence and conviction. Take credit for your strengths and make sure those who matter know it. Write weekly reports to your boss, meet with him or her on a regular basis to update your achievements and progress. No one else will do this for you! Keep it brief and to the point, and don't offer details unless asked. Don't worry about being self-promotional.

I have been in sales in one form or another for over 20 years, and I have learned how to sell myself. However I still have a little tiny voice in the back of my head that says "Wow! That sounds like I'm boasting, really stuck up, they're going to think I'm a real egomaniac!" So I've just learned to ignore it. In order to promote my services and programs, I have to be able to say with confidence, "This is what I've done for these companies, with these results. Over 95% of my business is repeat and referral, a clear sign of the excellent work I do for my clients."

Women, take credit for what you're good at
and make sure those who matter know it.

A participant in one of my workshops mentioned that she attended a class and read a book about grant writing. One of the things she learned was how to use more direct language regarding benefits and achievements because most of the people on the boards that approve grant money are men. Men expect good people to talk about their strengths; they have been programmed and socialized to do so. If men don't hear about specific strengths, they naturally assume that someone doesn't have those capabilities.

This perception of confidence by people in authority, particularly men, affects additional work areas. Not only are women promoted less, but their proposals are not approved as often as their male counterparts are because the boss views the women as less confident about what they are proposing.

## GENDERSMART CLUE:

Women, put yourselves in the boss' shoes for a moment. You have to select the next manager or the most effective proposal. Even with everything else equal, wouldn't you lean toward the person who seemed most confident about their abilities or ideas? "Seemed" is the operative word here. Men, recognize this style difference and consider it when making decisions involving personnel and project assignments.

Women, learn to publicize your strengths and accomplishments in an appropriate way. Learn how to communicate with confidence and resolve, how to sound like you know what you are doing and proposing. And support each other at all levels to help break the glass ceiling. Implementing the GenderSmart Clues throughout this book will help you with this adjustment.

# Discussing Problems and Feelings

Women discuss problems and feelings...they bond and process this way. Discussing problems and feelings is also a form of consensus building, another feminine style. But men, who don't discuss problems and feelings as a general rule, watch a woman talking about things that are bothering her, and think to themselves, "Yikes, she is a bottomless pit of problems, an emotional basketcase! She is going to fall apart here any minute!" Men, who process things internally, assume women are weak, too emotional, and troubled. And/or they think that women think men are responsible for the problem. "Gosh, she must be talking to me about this because she thinks it's my fault! I'd better do something about it."

Men, please remember that women simply share more and process out loud. Keep in mind the biological differences we covered previously, that women generally are more verbal than men. Talking through situations and feelings helps women sort things out and work through the emotion, in addition to creating rapport and bonding with the person they are processing with. Do women talk just to talk? You bet they do. And that's okay. It's just a style difference.

*"A closed mind is a dying mind."*

**Edna Ferber**

I notice myself expressing things verbally more and more often, as I get older. And I'm very comfortable admitting that I'm just yakking! Just talking, processing, sharing. I'm very verbal, sometimes I just plain and simple feel like yakking. It is important to note, however, that when in business situations I monitor that tendency to avoid being misperceived by men and labeled as weak or troubled or "too" talkative (as opposed to "more" talkative). Also, I try to watch body language so that if my listener's eyes glaze over with boredom I'll know when to wrap up. And, just as often, I don't feel like talking. Go figure.

We need to be aware not only of how we might be misperceiving others, but also of how we might be *being* misperceived so that we can adjust both our perceptions and our behavior. Each gender must take half of the responsibility for how we are perceived.

---

## GenderSmart Clue:

Men, discussing problems and feelings is a style difference, not necessarily a plea for help, an indication of fault, or an intentional effort to keep you from your work or news program. Women, be aware of how your verbal processing may be being perceived, and be selective of your timing and your audience.

---

# Handling Conflict

As mentioned in Chapter 4, women often avoid and fear conflict due to past programming. On the other hand, some women handle conflict well and don't shy from it when they feel it is necessary to further their careers or protect their projects and "turf." However, many still feel somewhat fearful and apprehensive about it, and often worry about the conflict after it takes place. They second-guess themselves, with questions like, "Will he be angry with me now?" "Did I just ruin my chances for the promotion?" "Do they think I'm a raving maniac after that last meeting?"

The conflict issue truly presents a fine line to toe for women. If they handle conflict indirectly, or avoid it, people (especially men, whose intuitive and people-reading skills are generally not as developed as women's) don't recognize that the conflict even exists. They can't read her mind...if she doesn't say anything or show discomfort or anger, how can they know?

Another perception involves women being perceived as less credible because men often recognize when conflict should happen. They notice when she should stand up for herself, and when she lets something go, or if she don't speak up when men would in a similar situation, she may be seen as a wimp.

A woman in one of my workshops said, "When I came into work this morning my boss said 'Hi dear', so I said 'Hi honey' so he'd know not to say that." I cautioned her, "Uh oh, you just gave him permission. Most likely, he is not going to understand that you don't like him calling you 'dear'. He's not going to get it; he won't recognize a conflict exists. I suggest you say to him, 'Please don't call me dear' or 'I would prefer that you call me Jill' or 'I appreciate your intention, I know you don't mean it in an offensive way, but I'd rather you call me by my name, okay? I like to keep terms like 'dear' reserved for my husband. Thanks for understanding."

........................................................................................................................

## Remember: directly, with compassion and grace.

........................................................................................................................

If women handle conflict very directly and firmly, then they're labeled bossy, bitchy, harsh, and witches. Here's where the fine line comes in. Indirectly...it doesn't work or backfires. Too directly...it blows up in your face. What do you do?

I recommend handling conflict directly but with compassion, just like the example with Jill above. Compassion does not mean sympathy in this context, but graciousness and respect. "I need your help with something, John. I work very hard to be taken seriously, and I don't want people to get the wrong impression by hearing others refer to me with terms of endearment. I know you don't mean to be offensive, and I appreciate that, but I'd really prefer that you call me Jill. Thanks for your help with this." That's polite and compassionate. He may be mildly shocked, but he'll get over it. You may need to remind him a couple times, which is fine. Remember this issue is far more important to you than to him.

Often when a woman comes across "too" harshly in others' opinions, it is a defensive reaction to not being taken seriously. When a woman doesn't feel heard or respected, she sometimes overreacts by pushing back in order to get attention and demand respect. Whatever the reason, and however understandable, the outcome is usually less than ideal.

## GenderSmart Clue:

**Remember the words: directly with compassion and grace. Be clear and polite; keep the goal in mind of maintaining the relationship. This approach will work for both sexes in most situations, and help avoid misunderstandings, confusion, and conflict. But if serious offenses take place, or repeated requests are ignored, a direct and firm approach is called for.**

## Nodding

Women often nod to let people know they are listening. Consequently, sometimes men interpret that women are agreeing with everything the men say. It can be confusing to men when women are nodding while listening, which to them means agreement and approval, then the women suddenly say "Absolutely not" or "I don't agree." Or, men think women are insincere because "she can't possibly agree with everything I say yet she's always nodding." Nodding is an active listener's way of saying "Yes, I'm listening, keep talking, I'm with you, okay, I understand, I'm hearing you." Whether or not they actually agree is a different story.

**GENDERSMART CLUE:**

Because nodding is a widespread form of active listening, and both men and women prefer active listening, I am not going to suggest that women stop nodding. At most, perhaps tone it down and say, "I understand" and "I see" from time to time. I also suggest that talkers simply learn to recognize that nodding is a sign of listening, not necessarily agreement.

## Adding Questions

Women, with more or less unconscious intentions of evading conflict, maintaining harmony, and avoiding "bossy" or demanding behavior, add questions to the end of their statements: "This is a good report, don't you think?" Deborah Tannen and Pat Heim, authors of books on gender communication, refer to these as "tag questions." To men, that approach or style sounds as if she is asking permission to think that the report is good, permission to have her opinion.

The more masculine style is "This is a good report", or more succinctly, "Good report." See the difference in perceived power of these statements? The softer style comes across to men as less credible and powerless, and they often mistakenly make the assumption that women are indecisive and weak management material. It's merely a style difference. Women have been programmed to be nice and sweet and unobtrusive, and that wiring permeates much of their communication.

**GENDERSMART CLUE:**

Women - use the more powerful version when expressing opinions or thoughts. Men - it's just a style that is different from yours.

# Sorry's and Disclaiming Phrases

Women, start counting your apologies. "Excuse me for interrupting" "Oh I'm sorry I forgot this page" "Oops, sorry, read the wrong line." Men don't apologize nearly this frequently. Start listening to your sorry's. Men hear these frequent apologies and assume weakness and subservient behavior. They are thinking, "Why is she always apologizing, she didn't do anything wrong." "She must be insecure or she lacks confidence." It's just another style difference.

Here is one situation where the genders would be better off meeting somewhere in the middle. Men, try to use more sorry's, and women, try to use fewer.

Expanding on the story I told in Chapter 5, during the same meeting with the president of the company, my friend Kris faced another unsavory experience. The president was challenging every attendee listed for the convention. He got to one name and stumbled over it while trying to pronounce it, asking whom the person was. Kris offered the correct pronunciation, and then added with a smile, "That happens to be me!" The president became flustered, and without apologizing, continued down the list. A better response? "Well, of course it's you!" with a slight smack to his forehead or some other self-deprecating body language to lightly acknowledge his goof.

The same applies to what I call disclaiming phrases and what Deborah Tannen and Pat Heim, authors of other books on gender issues, call disclaimers. "Well, this is just my opinion, but..." and "I don't know if this is right, but..." or "I may be out in left field here, but..." Who wants to hear or give credibility to what comes next? Those phrases dilute the power and confidence of your statements. Men, and women using a masculine communication style, see this approach as vague, wishy-washy, and less credible.

After over 20 years in a male-dominated business world, I have learned to state my opinion as fact. I make sure I sound confident and knowledgeable, and if I'm wrong I simply correct my statement. I learned that this method, even with making mistakes occasionally, was far more conducive to career enhancement than predicating my opinions with apologetic disclaimers.

## GenderSmart Clue:

Men, try not to assume "I'm sorry" means a women is admitting fault or apologizing. It's most likely simply a conversation-smoothing habit or routine. Perhaps consider using a few more sorry's yourselves. Women, be aware of the quantity of sorry's and disclaimers you use, and notice how they position you rather weakly in men's eyes.

## Indirect Requests

With the intention of avoiding conflict and "bossy" communication, women soften their requests. Remember, they've been programmed for consensus and harmony. Direct requests sound like snapping out orders to many women, making it difficult for them to give them. Consequently, men (and often some women) either feel manipulated or don't understand the point of the request, i.e., they don't "get it," basically rendering the query ineffective.

In the office for example, a female boss says to her assistant (male or female), "It sure would be nice to have this report by 10:00." The assistant thinks, "Let's see, okay, it would be nice by 10:00 but I've got these other two things to do, so 10:30 will probably be acceptable." He or she proudly turns the report in by 10:30 to a very unhappy boss, and both are upset. Both parties involved could have helped avoid this conflict and confusion.

First, the boss should be more direct when assigning a project. "I need this by 10:00, please. Thanks." Direct, clear, and also compassionate and polite with no rudeness or "bossiness." Second, the assistant should accept part of the responsibility and help clarify the deadline. "Is 10:00 the final deadline, or would 10:30 be okay because I've got these other two things to do?" Or, "I'm jammed with these other two projects, will you please help me prioritize them so I can be of the most help to you?" Conflict avoided, everyone's happy.

Another example: vague direction: "We've got to finish the Jones project." Clear direction: "Meeting the Jones project deadline is our top priority and it needs to be complete by Friday noon. Please update me on your progress by 4:00 this afternoon. Thanks."

So often, people internally question directions and instructions, wondering whether or not they understood everything accurately. But men, and also women concerned about being perceived as incompetent or less effective than their male co-workers, avoid asking questions to clarify. They think, "Gosh, I think this is what he meant, but if I ask a question he'll think I'm stupid or wasn't listening or that I don't understand the business." I think all supervisors will agree with me when I say that it is much better to clarify up front than waste time, effort and productivity heading off on an incorrect tangent.

---

Indirect communicators most likely have their hearts in the right place, but their words are not clear, resulting in ineffective requests and resentful recipients who feel confused or manipulated.

---

An interesting side note: In *Talking From 9 to 5*, Deborah Tannen reports that although direct communication is viewed in America as logical and preferred, varieties of indirectness are the norm in most other countries. Japanese anthropologist Takie Sugiyama Lebra explains that one of the most basic values in Japanese culture is omoiyari, which translates to empathy. This value implies that it should not be necessary to state one's meaning explicitly; people should be able to sense each other's meaning intuitively.

Indirect requests are also ineffective in personal situations. For example, a couple is driving along leisurely and the woman asks, "Are you hungry?" To her, she obviously meant, "I'm hungry, let's find a restaurant and pull over for lunch." To him, she merely asked if he was hungry. He is not, so he answers, "No" or "Not really' in an innocent, unsuspecting, and perfectly polite way. Next thing he knows, she is quiet and mildly upset, and he has no idea why. He's in trouble for honestly answering a question directed to him.

If you want something, just say so politely: "Honey, I'm hungry, let's get something to eat." He will be so relieved he doesn't have to try to decipher indirect innuendos. He won't feel manipulated. Yes, indirect communicators most likely have their hearts in the right place, but their words are not clear, resulting in ineffective requests and resentful recipients who feel confused or manipulated.

Is this a familiar scenario? "Oh look, the trash is full." Hubby walks by and says, "Yep, sure is." And he continues walking on by, while thinking, "I can tell she wants me to take out the trash, why doesn't she just ask me to take it out instead of hinting around like that? That drives me crazy! Why doesn't she just tell me what she wants?" Again, she's trying not to sound bossy or demanding. Her intentions are worthy. The effect is less desirable, however, so I suggest something like, "Honey, will you please take out the trash?" Or, just take it out herself.

> *"The only real mistake is the one from which we learn nothing."*
> **John Powell**

Even though I teach this information, at times I am guilty of indirect communication. Like I said, programming runs deep. I boarded a flight from Minneapolis to St. Louis recently, and found a pile of newspapers in my aisle seat. I stopped by the row, put my briefcase in the overhead compartment, stood there for a few seconds, and assumed the gentleman sitting in the window seat would notice me and move his papers from my seat. He didn't.

"Are those your papers?" I asked, obviously (to me) communicating, "Please move your papers so I can take my rightful seat.' He looked up and asked, "Is this your seat?" "Why else would I ask you to move them?" I thought to myself. I assumed he didn't want to be bothered and was making sure I had that seat. I half expected him to ask to see my boarding pass. "Yes", I answered deliberately, with a very slight air of Du-uh! Why else would I ask? He moved the papers and I sat down.

A few minutes later it hit me. He probably wondered if I wanted to take his used papers to read them for myself. After all, initially I merely asked him if they were his, I didn't ask him to move them. He was simply clarifying my indirect request, and confirming that the seat was indeed mine. Now the Duh! applies to me. Unbelievable how thorough this programming is with women. A better way of communicating that issue would have been with a friendly tone, "Hi, this is my seat. If those are your papers would you mind moving them? Thank you."

## GENDERSMART CLUE:

**Simply ask politely, in clear terms, for what you want. Be aware of your own and others' indirect communication and notice how it causes discomfort and confusion. Recognize the situations in which you find yourself trying to interpret or decipher what someone "really meant," where you are trying to "read between the lines." Frustrating, isn't it?**

## Expressing Emotion

In men's eyes, women are often too emotional. Let's look at it another way. Instead of expressing emotion *too* often, how about perceiving women as expressing emotion more often than men? Keep in mind that women have easier access to their emotions physiologically, and also have been told all their lives that it is perfectly acceptable and expected to cry and express their feelings.

Men have been programmed that expressing emotion (other than anger, a "masculine" emotion) is not acceptable, so women's emotions are confusing and threatening to them. Men feel compelled to stop the emotion because they have been wired to save the species, to fix things. They feel responsible. A popular song recites the line, "I die a little each time she cries." Also, some men feel manipulated, thinking women cry intentionally to get their way. Some do, probably, but I like to think a very small minority.

> *"To linger in the observation of things other than the self implies a profound conviction of their worth."*
> **Charles-Damian Boulogne**

If, for example, you are giving a woman a performance evaluation or review and she starts crying, hand her a tissue and keep talking. She can still hear you. Tell her you can see she is upset and ask how you can help or what the two of you need to discuss in more detail.

Usually, women cry in the office from tension, frustration, or not feeling understood and heard, not because they are sad or hurt. Remember the movie Courage Under Fire with Denzel Washington and Meg Ryan? Meg and her team were being fired on in the desert and she started crying. One of her men rolled his eyes and said, "Oh, terrific, now she's crying!" And she responded, "It's tension, you (bleep!)"

Various emotions come out as tears with women. Because men were wired to fix everything, and tears, to them, meant true doom, they are intimidated and frightened by this level of emotion.

Women have been told their entire lives that it is okay to cry. Because crying is not natural to men, her tears impact them much more than they bother her. Men don't necessarily need to do anything when she cries. In personal situations where touching is acceptable, simply holding her or softly stroking her arm or shoulder often adequately demonstrates that men care. When in doubt, ask!

The older I get, the more I cry. And the more comfortable I am with my tears. Not just sad tears, but happy tears, tears when I'm touched or moved emotionally, even by commercials!

## GENDERSMART CLUE:

Women generally are more emotional, just like men generally are more aggressive. Period. This is one of our wonderful differences to be celebrated. Men often like this softer side of women in personal situations, but they get even more confused when this characteristic surfaces at work. Emotion is purely a form of expression; it has nothing to do with management ability or intelligence.

# THE
# VIRTUES
# OF
# FLEXIBILITY

*"He who knows only his side of the case, knows little of that."*
**John Stuart Mill**

**Flexible** (FLEK se b'l) *adj. 1. capable of being bent, twisted, etc. 2. yielding; tractable. 3. able to adjust; adaptable. -flexibility n.*

*"There is, in sum, no one right way to be."*
**Carol Tavris, author of The Mismeasure of Woman**

The world tends to see things in opposites. In some ways I have fueled this perspective by referring to men and women as opposite sexes. I do it because I know most people are familiar and comfortable with this reference, and I would prefer that you read the book and understand its messages rather than put it down because you couldn't relate to its style. In addition, most women are definitely not men, and vice versa. So if we're not one, we must be the other. But this kind of opposition does not translate directly to the exclusive use of one or the other style of communication, in any given interaction.

As I've mentioned, differences exist not only between men and women, but also *among* men and women. In addition, differences abide between and among cultures, regions, religions, age groups, and other groups. This cacophony of differences is why there is no one right way of communicating, no one right style. Masculine and feminine styles are but two ways of making sense of differences, and this particular way of solving the communication puzzle works for the majority of people in North America and many other countries, but certainly not all.

Use this book as a simple way to understand gender communication differences, and know that other differences also play into communication success. "GenderSmart®" will definitely help you solve the communication puzzle between men and women. Being flexible in your interactions with others will help keep the puzzle pieces in place.

*"Flexibility is the key to success – along with mutual respect."*
**Deborah Tannen, Talking From 9 to 5**

As Tannen says, there is no one best way. Any style of speaking will work in many situations, if those you are speaking with share your style. Even then, misunderstandings will occur due to conflicts of interest, the speaker's or listener's mood, frame of reference, etc. Bottom line, if your goal is truly communication – to understand and be understood – then it's not enough for the language to be right; the style of communication needs to be shared, or at least understood.

In the workplace, people of different ethnic and class backgrounds, from different areas of the country and the world – combined with all of their different personalities – obviously results in a plethora of conversational styles. Organizations that have a "good-style" model will create a staff well-trained to perform successfully with individuals – customers and co-workers – with some similar styles, but those who do not subscribe to that style will be alienated. The company that accommodates employees with a range of styles will have far more flexibility and therefore success with customers and other staff members with varying styles.

When we have differing conversational styles, our good intentions may not be enough. This is why, as a communicator, active listening skills and observation of facial expressions and body language are so vital to clear and successful communication. This is also why it is important as a listener to ask questions and clarify anything that doesn't ring true, make sense, or meet our expectations. It takes two to tango, at least to tango well.

*"You take people as far as they will go, not as far as you would like them to go."*
**Jeannette Rankin**

So many people think that women's style is better, or men's style is better. I prefer my own style, as it makes the most sense to me because I am most familiar with it compared to any other style. Likewise, you probably prefer your own style. And that's fine. What's key to realize, though, is that no style is better. They are all valid as styles, and each one works best with others who share similar styles. But no one style will work in every situation, so ultimately, the best style is a flexible one that can respond to other's differences.

For example, in the Tips For Men section of the Chapter 8, I advise men to reduce the number of sports metaphors they commonly use in conversation. Following are a few of these metaphors. Try filling in the blanks with other ways to express the same thought:

**Sports Metaphor**                                      **Another expression**

1.  If this doesn't work,
    we'll have to punt.                    _____

2.  It's a fourth down situation.          _____

3.  The ball is in your court.             _____

4.  Let's take a time out.                 _____

5.  He just sits on the sidelines.         _____

6.  Who dropped the ball?                  _____

7.  Let's dangle some bait and
    see if he bites.                       _____

8.  He scored big time on that one.        _____

9.  Yes! A home run!                       _____

10. Are you in this game or not?           _____

Gender influences are but one foundation of differences, albeit a powerful one, that when understood and incorporated into conversation will definitely help improve communication between men and women. The cautions in this chapter are by no means meant to imply that clear and successful communication is impossible unless you know the impact of all existing conversational styles. My intention is to communicate that flexibility is always beneficial to successful communication and can take the virtues of gender difference understanding to an even higher level.

*"As long as the question is framed this way – 'What can we do about them, the other, the opposite?' – it can never be answered, no matter which sex is being regarded as 'them.' The question, rather, should be this: What shall we do about us, so that our relationships, our work, our children, and our planet with flourish?"*

**Carol Tavris, The Mismeasure of Woman**

CHAPTER

# 8

# KEY POINTS
# AND TIPS

*"The hardest of all is learning to be a well of affection,
and not a fountain; to show them we love them not when
we feel like it, but when they do."*
**Nan Fairbrother**

For your convenience, the key messages in this book are outlined below. For ease of referral, I have also listed the primary gender communication differences with the reasons these differences exist, their source and rationale (primarily the status vs. connection issue), both biological and social programming. In addition, this chapter includes a few tips for men and women to help solve the communication puzzle between the sexes.

- Men and women are different! Ignoring differences will only escalate resentment and confusion.

- By understanding what these differences are and how they manifest in communication and interaction, men and women can work and live together much more harmoniously.

- Differences are evolutionary and social, and both are intertwined. The sexes were programmed for varying tasks and responsibilities to ensure survival of the species. Both nature and nurture have created style differences.

- Men and women don't need each other to stay alive, as they did in the past. At some deep level, this lack of feeling needed is threatening, especially to men.

- However, on the other hand, men and women do need each other to maintain the species, and dependency in any situation often causes resentment.

- Give people the benefit of the doubt before jumping to conclusions that they are intentionally trying to be offensive. Evaluate their meaning and intention.

- Be flexible. Differences not only exist between men and women, but also among men and among women, between cultures, religions, regions, age groups, geographical areas, and more.

- Maintain a positive attitude. Celebrate and be grateful for our differences, and for the fact that we are not like the Macintosh lemmings commercial from years past where people looked and acted the same and had no individuality or diversity. Be aware of, respect, and learn about our differences. A positive attitude is paramount to avoiding and resolving negative gender communication issues.

**These key points can also be expressed through my G-E-N-D-E-R acronym:**

# G o for understanding and acceptance

# E xamine masculine and feminine styles

# N otice your perceptions of others' styles

# D iscover how others may perceive you

# E nrich relationships with this knowledge

# R etain flexibility and an open dialogue

| MEN'S (Masculine) STYLE | EXISTENCE RATIONALE / REASONS |
|---|---|
| Discuss problems infrequently | Independence, superiority, less verbal |
| Talk to fix and solve problems, brief, focused, few details | Superiority, less verbal, don't bond through talking, wired to "save lives" |
| Don't give same emotional support | Less access to emotions, superiority, not as relationship-oriented, independent |
| Listen silently | Process internally, less verbal, less eye contact |
| Avoid constant, direct eye contact | Avoiding aggression, avoiding flirting |
| Use aggressive humor and put-downs | Superiority, competition, bonding style |
| Take more physical space | Superiority, competition, larger bodies |
| Make decisions independently | Independence, superiority |
| "Do this" "give me this" | Superiority, pyramid hierarchy, direct |
| "Girl," "honey," "doll," "gal" etc. | Superiority, habit, not detail-oriented, (forget names) |

| WOMEN'S (Feminine) STYLE | EXISTENCE RATIONALE / REASONS |
|---|---|
| Discuss decisions, "Let's do this," "How about this" | Consensus, harmony, inclusive approach, avoid giving orders, equal hierarchy |
| Use apologies, tag questions, disclaimers | Consensus, harmony, downplaying own authority |
| Don't boast or sell themselves | Maintain even hierarchy, harmony, relationships |
| Discuss problems and feelings | More verbal, bond through talking and sharing, easier access to emotions |
| Avoid or fear conflict | Consensus, harmony, survival |
| Make indirect requests | Harmony, avoid orders, maintain level hierarchy |
| Use fewer open postures | "Be ladylike," harmony, less competitive, less territorial |
| Cry and express emotions | Socially okay, wired for emotional impact and memory |

# TIPS FOR WOMEN SPEAKING TO MEN
# OR FEMININE STYLE TO MASCULINE STYLE

1. Be clear, direct, and polite with requests and assignments.
2. Add business terminology and power to words.
3. Reduce superlatives such as wonderful, beautiful, fantastic, etc.
4. Be brief and specific unless more details have been requested.
5. Speak with confidence and authority, i.e., make statements, don't ask permission for your opinion or direction (see #6)
6. Monitor use of "Don't you agree?" "What if we do it this way?" etc.
7. Handle conflict directly and clearly, with compassion and courtesy.
8. When interrupted, courteously use direct language and take the floor back.
9. Don't try to be "one of the boys."
10. Remember you don't have to like someone to get the job done.
11. Recognize that others' intentions may be different than your perceptions of their words or behavior.
12. As a manager, focus on key leverage work; don't get mired in details. Delegate.
13. Promote your strengths, skills, and accomplishments within your organization with regular briefings, reports, etc.
14. Monitor amount of people, feelings, relationships talk content.
15. Maintain a professional, well-groomed appearance and image.
16. Use more literal terms, say what you mean, no hinting around.
17. Make some decisions independently rather than always asking others for their input.
18. Don't assume men are intentionally being offensive.
19. Avoid strong displays of emotion.
20. Reduce the number of times you say, "I'm sorry."

21. Pick your battles - don't fight every little offense - one step at a time.

22. Be flexible and keep a positive attitude about differences!

## TIPS FOR MEN SPEAKING TO WOMEN
## OR MASCULINE STYLE TO FEMININE STYLE

1.  Be aware that the impact and perception of your communication may be negative, regardless of your good intentions.

2.  Add a little feeling and relationship talk content.

3.  Use a win-win style, not win-lose or one-up. Be aware of which style you're using.

4.  Use "woman" and "women" or genderless terms, such as "everyone," "managers," "people," "technicians," etc.

5.  Recognize that her intentions may be different than your perception of her words or behavior.

6.  Monitor use of "Do this," "Give me that," and other abrasive language.

7.  Use "I'm sorry" "Pardon me" "Please" and "Thank you" more often.

8.  Use general humor - with occasional self put-downs - not aggressive, offensive, sexual humor or put-downs of others.

9.  A woman's (or man's) softer style does not necessarily mean a less competent person.

10. If women discuss problems with you, ask if they want help or if they prefer just a listener.

11. Remember you are not responsible for their problems.

12. Be empathetic but not afraid of women's crying; it's just a different way of expressing emotion.

13. Ask women for their opinions and input more often.

14. Be aware that many women prefer more detail, and be prepared to

offer it.

15. Maintain a professional, well-groomed appearance and image.

16. Be personable and insert a little personal disclosure.

17. Maintain direct, but not constant, eye contact.

18. Avoid interrupting and use active listening skills.

19. Watch facial expressions and body language for signs of upset or confusion.

20. Say "I'm sorry" more often, including for small mistakes or offenses.

21. Don't underestimate a woman's capabilities just because she doesn't talk about her accomplishments and strengths.

22. Be flexible and keep a positive attitude about differences!

*"The important thing is to not stop questioning."*
**Albert Einstein**

CHAPTER

9

PRACTICE!

*"I hear and I forget. I see and I remember. I do and I understand."*
**Confucius**

**W**hy not practice what you've learned? Completing these exercises will help integrate your learning into your interaction with others, in several different yet common situations, both at work and at home. Once you work them out, you'll have them for reference and application to similar real-life circumstances.

Remember, there is no one perfectly right way, especially because in a few of the case studies there are ambiguities where you will need to make some assumptions. Also keep in mind that there are always two sides to every situation. Just have fun with them. It might help to pause after reading each one and put yourself in the characters' shoes. Refer back to the information in the book. At the end of the chapter I have included scripts for a few of the situations to help you confirm direction and check your ideas, however your script should be in your words. And remember, there are as many right answers as there are people to give them!

**A few tips:**

1. Compassionate and polite are usually the best approaches.
2. Every situation has two valid sides.
3. Be clear, succinct, and describe feelings.
4. Ask for support or behavior you want.
5. People often respond defensively when they feel attacked, unloved, or disrespected. Keep them feeling safe and your interactions will be much more successful and pleasant.
6. The more specific you are with scripting responses in this exercise, the better prepared you will be to handle communication conflicts more effectively in real life.

*"Nothing strengthens the judgment and quickens
the conscience like individual responsibility."*
**Elizabeth Cady Stanton**

# I. THE MEETING

Every Tuesday morning, Louis, John, Marjorie, Howard, and Keith meet to discuss current project status. During the most recent meeting, Marjorie made a suggestion for a procedural change. No one responded, so she assumed they didn't like the idea.

Later in the meeting, Louis made the same suggestion and the group acknowledged and discussed it, and with a few small revisions, accepted it. Louis was thanked for his valuable contribution, while Marjorie remained silent, shocked and upset that she was ignored when she offered the same idea earlier.

1. What gender differences may have contributed to this situation?

2. What could the others have done differently to acknowledge and be fair to Marjorie? Be specific with scripts as requested below.

   a. What could Louis have said? How could he have presented the same idea later?

   b. How about John, Howard and Keith?

3. How could Marjorie have handled it?

   a. How could she have prefaced her suggestion and presented it to the group?

   b. What might she have said when Louis voiced the same idea later?

## II. THE ABSENT LISTENER

Patty had a lot on her mind, and she really needed to vent. Bruce listened while browsing through the trader ads – he was looking for a used car.

"Have you heard a word I've said?" Patty exclaimed. "You never listen to me, I don't think you even care what I say or what bothers me. How can you treat me like that!" Bruce looked annoyed and didn't know how to respond. "I heard you, what's the big deal?" Patty's jaw dropped at what she felt to be such an insensitive remark. She left the room in tears.

1. What gender differences may have contributed to this situation?

2. What could Bruce have done differently while Patty was talking to him?

3. How could Patty have better discussed her concerns with Bruce?

## III. THE EXCLUSION

Jessica couldn't believe it. The other members of the task force, Jeff, Ralph, and Linda, left her out of an important meeting again. This had happened before. The group did not notify her of the meeting and important decisions were made without her.

Jeff was her contact point. He was supposed to inform her of all meetings. The last time she was left out, Jessica told Jeff she felt excluded and hurt, and asked him to please include her in the future. He did for the next few weeks, but now it looked like he was back to old tricks. Didn't the other two, Ralph and Linda, wonder where she was during these meetings? What were they thinking?

1. What gender differences may have contributed to this situation?

2. What should Jessica do? What exactly should she say, to whom?

3. Any other suggestions?

# IV. THE GRUFF CLIENT

Nancy, a sales rep with Finest Forms, is intimidated by Hank, who works for one of her largest customers. Hank is a purchasing agent with Best Bank. He responded gruffly when Nancy tried to interview him regarding specific needs for the bank's new forms system. He cut answers short and wouldn't take the time to provide the details Nancy needed, to ensure a quality and accurate job. Hank often said, "Whatever!" or other similar brush-offs instead of answering Nancy's questions completely and clearly. Finally, he told her it was her job to figure out the details, that's part of what he's paying for.

Nancy left and drove back to the office. She was frustrated, embarrassed, angry, and concerned about producing the new system accurately and timely. Hank was a jerk! But she had to get the information from him regardless of her feelings and opinions. She called Hank's assistant and made an appointment for the next day. Now what?

1. What gender differences may have contributed to this situation?

With Hank?

With Nancy?

2. What can Nancy say to Hank to help him understand the importance of his cooperation? How should she approach him, in terms of tone and manner? Be specific with a detailed script that can be acted out for the group.

3. What can Nancy do to prevent this delay/obstacle from happening again in the future, with Hank or anyone else?

# V. THE RIDE

Frank was looking forward to his horseback ride. It had been years since he was last on a horse and he missed it. As he walked over the hill to where the wrangler was grooming the horses, he called out hello.

"Hi!" responded Betty the wrangler. "You must be Frank. Welcome to Fast Gallop Ranch. Tell me what kind of riding you do, and how often, so I can pick the right horse for you."

"Oh, I prefer Western, and I've ridden quite a bit. Since I was a kid, actually. I'm pretty comfortable on a horse, please don't give me an old nag or anything like that."

"You got it!" Betty said. She saddled up Lady for her customer and took Frank out on a ride in the canyon.

During the ride, Betty could see that Frank was not steady and balanced in the saddle, so she opted not to canter. Frank was disappointed and complained to Cathy, the ranch's owner, when they returned to the barn. "How long has it been since you've ridden? Cathy asked. "Tell me again exactly how much riding you have done. Our first concern here is safety, and if Betty didn't feel you would have been safe going at a faster gait, or if she thought that Lady was the wrong horse for you, then I trust her decision. I'm very sorry your ride didn't meet your expectations, we sure want everyone to have fun here. Why not come back again, and we'll schedule a short refresher lesson for you before taking you out into the canyon. How does that sound?" Frank seemed pacified, scheduled the next ride, and left.

1. What gender differences may have contributed to this situation?

2. How could Frank have avoided his disappointment?

3. What could Betty have done differently before she selected Lady for Frank?

4. What could Frank have said during the ride to make both he and Betty more comfortable?

5. What could Betty have said during the ride?

# VI. THE MENTOR AND PROTÉGÉ

Claire is an experienced new hire with the firm and Rob, her mentor, has been guiding her for several months. To date, general mentoring principles such as Claire's objectives and available resources have been addressed, along with some advice regarding client issues.

As one aspect of his mentoring responsibilities, Rob has been observing Claire in her interactions during meetings (both formal and informal) and with clients and co-workers. He noticed that she has a tendency to ask many questions to get input for decisions, even from "lower level" staff. As a matter of fact, Rob overheard a male partner remark, "We hired Claire for her expertise and answers, why is she always asking for help? Doesn't she know what she's doing?"

Rob feels Claire has the ability to advance in the firm, but doubts her potential if this behavior continues. To his chagrin, after procrastinating for several weeks, he must address Claire's behavior during their next meeting.

1.  What gender differences may have contributed to this situation? And why would Rob have procrastinated giving his feedback to Claire?

2. How should Rob handle this? Prepare specific script.

3. How would the script change if Claire's mentor were a woman?

4. How would Rob's approach be different if Claire's style was just the opposite, too aggressive and non-inclusive?

## VII. THE REMARKS

Jennifer is a new receptionist at a major automobile dealership. She is in her early 20s, is intelligent and has good potential, but is still "learning the ropes."

Mary is a senior sales representative in her early 50s whom Jennifer respects and knows she can learn from. However, Mary regularly does something that annoys Jennifer...she calls her "Dear" and "Hon" and only uses Jennifer's name when she needs to get her attention from across the floor.

Jennifer is becoming increasingly resentful about this, and it is beginning to affect her working relationship with Mary. She hinted (by imitating Mary and rolling her eyes) to Paul, her boss that Mary's remarks were patronizing, but Paul just laughed and continued on with his work.

1. What gender differences (Jennifer, Mary, and Paul) may be contributing to this situation?

2. How should Jennifer deal with Mary? Prepare specific script.

3.  What could Jennifer have done to avoid her resentment?

4.  What should Jennifer have said to Paul, if anything, and when?

5.  Given Jennifer's approach to Paul, what could he have done differently to help Jennifer's situation? Please be specific.

# VIII. THE TALKER

Helen is an experienced customer service rep who has been with her employer for eight years now. George, her sales counterpart, is a partner with the company and has been in the business for 15 years. But George, and for that matter, many of Helen's co-workers, often avoid conversations with her. In their view, Helen talks too much. She always launches into great detail about aspects of the business or other topic at hand, and takes up too much time. To make matters worse, once in a while her lengthy descriptions end up taking even more time because her listener is confused by the detail and needs further explanation.

George dreads the times he and Helen work together on a job. He has already tried hinting around, and has tried to look busy, having his assistant page him. He has even politely asked Helen to get to the point because he had a meeting to go to and wanted to help her with her questions first. Nothing has worked. But now that Helen's co-workers are complaining, he must do something more effective. Talking with her supervisor is not an option for personal reasons.

1.  What gender differences may have contributed to this situation?

With Helen?

With George?

2.  What should George say to Helen? Which response style(s) would be most appropriate? Write a specific script that can be acted out for the group.

3.  What could Helen's co-workers say to her to help her understand the situation?

4.  How should Helen report or discuss matters of importance to her?

# IX. THE ARGUMENT

Ryan came home Wednesday night, an hour later than his wife Julie expected. She was upset. "Why are you always late? Why didn't you call me? I thought something bad might have happened! What am I supposed to think when you're late like this?"

"Sometimes things don't work out the way you want them to, Julie!" Ryan responded defensively. "I can't live my life to satisfy your every desire." He stormed off into his den and closed the door.

1. What gender differences may have contributed to this situation?

2. How should Julie have handled the situation?

3. What could Ryan have done differently?

4. What can this couple do now and in the future to avoid this type of argument?

# X. THE TEMPER

Nicole, known for her sweet, gregarious personality, is a vehicle sales representative. She often partners with Tom, a sales representative with about six month's more experience.

Nicole was working with a prospective buyer who, after three visits to the dealership, decided against buying an Explorer. Tom lost his temper at Nicole and yelled at her, blaming her for the lost sale. Everyone could see that Nicole was embarrassed and upset. She avoided Tom the rest of the day. The next day she talked to several of her co-workers about what a jerk Tom was.

1. What gender differences may have contributed to this situation?




2. How should Nicole have handled it? Be specific with response style(s) and script.

   a. When Tom yelled at her?




   b. The next day?

3. What should Tom have done differently? Be specific with response style and script.

    a. Rather than yell at Nicole?

    b. When he noticed that Nicole was upset?

# XI. THE PROJECT

Eric, a new hire with the Firm, is eager to get started on his first scheduled project the Monday after his orientation. Unfortunately, Ashley, the senior on the job, is on vacation for the next two weeks. On advice from a second year associate, Mary, he decides to get started on the project and refers to Mary for questions.

Prior to starting, however, he leaves Ashley a voicemail letting her know he is starting the project. Two weeks later, Eric is proud to present the project to Ashley, which he believes to be 80% complete using only 60% of budgeted time. Ashley begins to berate him for 10 minutes, telling him he had used poor judgment, and asks him "how could you have started this project without first asking me?" Eric becomes very upset. He was only trying to meet his goal and is even more enraged when he receives negative feedback on only four minor points on the project after Ashley's review. "Besides, she never responded to my voicemail!"

1. What gender differences may have contributed to this situation?

2. How should Ashley have handled the situation?
   a. When she first found out about it?

   b. After she reviewed the work?

3. What could Eric have done differently?
   a. When Mary recommended he go ahead and get started?

   b. When Ashley didn't respond to his message?

4. Is the relationship reconcilable? How so?
   a. Between Ashley and Eric?

   b. Between Eric and Mary?

# XII. THE SPENDAHOLIC

Van reviewed the credit card statement and stormed into the kitchen. "Charlotte, what is the matter with you? I've told you a thousand times to stop buying all this household stuff! Don't you get it, we're on a tight budget! How do you expect to be able to send the kids to college if you keep spending our money on towels and knick-knacks?"

Charlotte looked frustrated and guilty at the same time. She sighed and went into the bedroom, with no response. Van's anger only grew.

1. What gender differences may have contributed to this situation?

2. What could Van have said differently to keep Charlotte engaged in the discussion?

3. How could Charlotte have responded differently to Van?

4. What can this couple do differently next time one of them have a major concern about the other's behavior?

# XIII. THE FINANCIAL PLANNER

Cindi was considering resigning. Her job as a financial planner was difficult enough as it was without the daily struggle for her manager's attention. She worked long hours and tried very hard, but there was so much to learn and she felt she needed more guidance in order to provide the best service, products, and plans for her clients.

Her manager Rashid was busy too, and did not (would not? could not?) give her the time she needed. He would swing by her desk every day or so and ask, "How's it going?" However, because he kept walking or otherwise always looked to be in a hurry, Cindi could tell he hoped she would say only, "Great!" On the rare occasions when she did get some one-on-one time with him in his office, he would say something like, "Okay let's dive in and figure out what you're doing wrong."

Again, she was frustrated and just about ready to quit. Her manager didn't understand her or her needs.

1.  What gender differences may be contributing to this situation?

2.  How could Rashid interact more effectively with Cindi?

3. What would be a better way for Rashid to address Cindi's challenges?

4. What could Cindi say to Rashid to get more effective and productive attention and guidance from him?

# SUGGESTED RESPONSES

## I. THE MEETING

Every Tuesday morning, Louis, John, Marjorie, Howard, and Keith meet to discuss current project status. During the most recent meeting, Marjorie made a suggestion for a procedural change. No one responded, so she assumed they didn't like the idea.

Later in the meeting, Louis made the same suggestion and the group acknowledged and discussed it, and with a few small revisions, accepted it. Louis was thanked for his valuable contribution, while Marjorie remained silent, shocked and upset that she was ignored when she offered the same idea earlier.

1. What gender differences may have contributed to this situation? Men – superiority, independence, competition, less attention to detail; Women – inclusive and indirect language, avoid conflict, don't boast or take credit, harmony, inferiority.

2. What could the others have done differently to acknowledge and be fair to Marjorie? Be specific with scripts.

    a. What could Louis have said? How could he have presented the same idea later? "Marjorie, great idea. I was thinking the same thing and have a couple additions." Or "Marjorie's earlier idea was a good one. Let's expand on that concept."

    b. How about John, Howard and Keith? "Yes, Louis, that's what Marjorie was talking about earlier." Or "Marjorie is that basically what you mentioned before?"

3. How could Marjorie have handled it?

    a. How could she have prefaced her suggestion and presented it to the group? "I have an idea, let's..." Or "You guys will like this idea," Or "I've got a good idea, here it goes..."

    b. What might she have said when Louis voiced the same idea

later? "Yes, Louis, that's what I was talking about earlier," Or "Great minds think alike, my thoughts exactly, Louis."

## II. THE ABSENT LISTENER

Patty had a lot on her mind, and she really needed to vent. Bruce listened while browsing through the trader ads – he was looking for a used car.

"Have you heard a word I've said?" Patty exclaimed. "You never listen to me, I don't think you even care what I say or what bothers me. How can you treat me like that!" Bruce looked annoyed and didn't know how to respond. "I heard you, what's the big deal?" Patty's jaw dropped at what she felt to be such an insensitive remark. She left the room in tears.

1.  What gender differences may have contributed to this situation? Men – less attention to detail, bond through tasks and activities, feel responsible for women's felings, feel attacked, silent listening; Women – bond through talking, process verbally, need eye contact, more attuned to emotions, need more emotional support

2.  What could Bruce have done differently while Patty was talking to him? Establish better eye contact, nod and insert "I understand," "wow," or something similar every once in a while, ask her questions about what she is saying and how she is feeling.

3.  How could Patty have better discussed her concerns with Bruce? Before starting the discussion - "Bruce, I need to talk about something and I'd really appreciate your full attention. It always helps me to talk things over with you, you can be a really good listener." After Bruce wasn't listening – "Bruce, this is important to me. I know you need to read the ads but I'd really appreciate you waiting to do that for just a few minutes while we talk."

# V. THE RIDE

Frank was looking forward to his horseback ride. It had been years since he was last on a horse and he missed it. As he walked over the hill to where the wrangler was grooming the horses, he called out hello.

"Hi!" responded Betty the wrangler. "You must be Frank. Welcome to Fast Gallop Ranch. Tell me what kind of riding you do, and how often, so I can pick the right horse for you."

"Oh, I prefer Western, and I've ridden quite a bit. Since I was a kid, actually. I'm pretty comfortable on a horse, please don't give me an old nag or anything like that."

"You got it!" Betty said. She saddled up Lady for her customer and took Frank out on a ride in the canyon.

During the ride, Betty could see that Frank was not steady and balanced in the saddle, so she opted not to canter. Frank was disappointed and complained to Cathy, the ranch's owner, when they returned to the barn. "How long has it been since you've ridden? Cathy asked. "Tell me again exactly how much riding you have done. Our first concern here is safety, and if Betty didn't feel you would have been safe going at a faster gait, or if she thought that Lady was the wrong horse for you, then I trust her decision. I'm very sorry your ride didn't meet your expectations, we sure want everyone to have fun here. Why not come back again, and we'll schedule a short refresher lesson for you before taking you out into the canyon. How does that sound?" Frank seemed pacified, scheduled the next ride, and left.

1. What gender differences may have contributed to this situation? Men – superiority, independence, competition; Women – harmony, avoid conflict

2. How could Frank have avoided his disappointment? He should have been more honest and thorough about his riding ability up front. Ask Betty for some tips while riding. Admit he's a little out of practice and ask her if it's possible to change horses to one with

a smoother gait.

3. What could Betty have done differently before she selected Lady for Frank? "Frank, when you say you've ridden a lot, how much exactly? How often and how long ago? Are you comfortable cantering? Usually what we do here is see how the ride is going before we decide how much cantering we can do, okay? Safety's most important. And we want to have lots of fun too!"

4. What could Frank have said during the ride to make both he and Betty more comfortable? "Betty, I guess I'm a little rusty, can you give me some pointers? What do I need to do so we can canter?"

5. What could Betty have said during the ride? "Frank, maybe it's been longer than you remembered since you've ridden regularly. Lady has a big canter and I'm not sure she's the best horse for you. Can I give you a couple tips to make your ride more comfortable?" Or "I'm not sure it's safe to canter today, you might be a little out of practice and we sure don't want to get anyone hurt. Next time we'll put you on Princess and you'll be more comfortable. Then we can canter a lot."

## VII. THE REMARKS

Jennifer is a new receptionist at a major automobile dealership. She is in her early 20s, is intelligent and has good potential, but is still "learning the ropes."

Mary is a senior sales representative in her early 50s whom Jennifer respects and knows she can learn from. However, Mary regularly does something that annoys Jennifer...she calls her "Dear" and "Hon" and only uses Jennifer's name when she needs to get her attention from across the floor.

Jennifer is becoming increasingly resentful about this, and it is beginning to affect her working relationship with Mary. She hinted (by imitating Mary and rolling her eyes) to Paul, her boss that Mary's remarks were patronizing, but Paul just laughed and continued on with his work.

1. What gender differences (Jennifer, Mary, and Paul) may be contributing to this situation? Men/masculine style – less harmony, emotion, relationship orientation, less desire for details, independence, superiority (wants them to handle it themselves); Women – indirect, avoid conflict, inferior.

2. How should Jennifer deal with Mary? Prepare specific script. "Mary, I'm learning so much from you and I'm grateful for your help. There's another thing I could use your help with too. I know you mean well, but I'd really appreciate it if you would call me Jennifer all the time instead of 'dear' and 'hon.' It may seem small but it's important to me. Can you help me with that?"

3. What could Jennifer have done to avoid her resentment? Speak with Mary about it right away instead of waiting.

4. What should Jennifer have said to Paul, if anything, and when? She should have handled the situation with Mary, and gone to Paul only if Mary's behavior didn't change after a few requests. If she did need to talk to Paul about it, "Paul, I need your help with a

situation. It's not life or death, but important enough for me to talk with you about it. Mary keeps calling me 'dear' and 'hon' and I'm a little offended by that. I've talked to her a couple times but nothing has changed. Mary helps me a lot, I don't want to hurt our relationship. Is there some way you could help me out? How about making a general announcement in our next staff meeting, reminding everyone of the company's policies?"

5. Given Jennifer's approach to Paul, what could he have done differently to help her situation? Please be specific.

When in doubt, ask. Paul noticed that Jennifer's imitating Mary was unusual, and he could have asked Jennifer if she was just playing around or if something was bothering her that she wanted to talk about. He then could have given her suggestions as to how to handle it with Mary, or make the announcement Jennifer suggested, or handle it as he felt most appropriate.

**Note:** Remember that the objectives of handling these relatively low levels of conflict include maintaining the relationship and taking into consideration the personality and style of the other people involved. Unless the offense is major, career-threatening, or repetitive, a harmonious approach most likely will be most effective. Describe the problem, why it is of concern, and the changes you need with diplomacy, respect, and compassion. At the same time be clear and concise – no hints.

However, if the offense is major, career-threatening, or continues after repeated attempts to diffuse the behavior, then a more direct, assertive approach, possibly with notification that superiors will be advised of the issue if it is not resolved, is called for and warranted.

# BIBLIOGRAPHY

## Books:

Baridon, A.P. and Eyler, D.R. *Working Together.* New York: McGraw-Hill, Inc., 1994.

Beckwith, S. *Why Can't a Man Be More Like a Woman?* New York: Kensington Books, 1995.

Bly, R. Iron John, *A Book About Men.* Addison-Wesley Publishing Company, Inc., 1990.

Briles, Judith. *Gender Traps.* New York: McGraw Hill, 1996.

Brizendine, Louann, MD, *The Female Brain.* Morgan Road Books, 2006.

Evatt, Cris. *The Opposite Sides Of The Bed.* Emeryville, CA: Conari Press, 1993.

Fyock, C.D. *Women In The Workplace.* San Diego: Pfeiffer & Company, 1994.

Glass, L. Ph.D. *He Says, She Says.* New York: Perigee Books, 1992. (310) 274-0528.

Gray, J. *Men Are From Mars, Women Are From Venus.* New York: HarperCollins Publishers, 1992. (800) 821-3033

Hart, L.B. and Dalke, D. *The Sexes At Work.* Amherst, MA: HRD Press, Inc., 1992.

Heim, Pat Ph.D. *Smashing The Glass Ceiling.* New York: Fireside (Simon & Schuster), 1993.

Lightle, J. and Doucet, B. *Sexual Harassment In The Workplace.* Menlo Park, CA: Crisp Publications, Inc., 1992. (800) 442-7477.

Manning, M. and Haddock, P. *Leadership Skills For Women.* Menlo Park, CA: Crisp Publications, Inc., 1989.

Melia, J. *Breaking Into the Boardroom.* New York: G. Putnam's Sons, 1986.

Miles, Rosalind. *The Women's History of the World.* Salem House Publishers, 1989.

Morgan, Elaine. *The Descent of Woman*. New York, Stein and Day Publishers, 1972.

Myers, S. and Lambert, J. *Gender At Work*; Improving Relationships, 1992. (619) 755-3160.

Reardon, Kathleen Kelley, Ph.D. *They Don't Get It, Do They?* Little, Brown and Company, 1995.

Schaef, A.W. *Women's Reality*. Harper San Francisco, 1992.

Simons, G. and Weissman, G.D. *Men and Women, Partners at Work*. Menlo Park, CA: Crisp Publications, Inc., 1990. (800) 442-7477.

Steinem, G. *Revolution From Within*. Canada: Little, Brown & Company, 1993.

Tanenbaum, J. *Male & Female Realities*. Chicago: IPG, 1989. (800) 888-4741.

Tannen, D. *Talking From 9 to 5*. New York: William Morrow & Company, 1994.

Tannen, D. *You Just Don't Understand, Women and Men In Conversation*. New York: Ballantine Books, 1990. (800) 733-3000.

Tavris, Carol. *The Mismeasure of Woman*. Touchstone Books, Simon & Schuster, 1992.

Tingley, J. Genderflex – *Ending The Workplace War Between The Sexes*. Phoenix: Performance Improvement Pros, 1993. (800) 795- 4346.

White, Jane *A Few Good Women: Breaking The Barriers To Top Management*. Prentice Hall 1990.

## Articles:

Alperstein, Ellen. "Say Cheese. New Research Tracks the 'Grin Gap' Between Boys and Girls." *Los Angeles Times*, April 14, 2000.

Baird, J.E. and Bradley, P.H. "Styles of Management and Communication: A Comparative Study of Men and Women." *Communication Monographs*, Volume 46, June 1979.

Brotman, Barbara "When a Woman Blows the Whistle." Reprinted from the *Chicago Tribune by the Los Angeles Times*, Spring 2002.

Brothers, J. "What Men Don't Understand About Women." *Reader's Digest*, July 1994.

Brownell, J. "Communicating With Credibility: The Gender Gap." *The Cornell H.R.A.* Quarterly, April 1993.

Caudron, Shari. "Sexual Politics (Gender Relations In The Office)." *Personnel Journal*, v74n5, p. 50, May 1995.

Chusmir, L.H. and Parker, B. "Gender and Situational Differences in Managers' Values: A Look at Work and Home Lives." *Journal of Business Research*, 1991:23:325-335.

Epstein, C.F. "Ways Men and Women Lead." *Harvard Business Review*, Jan-Feb 1991.

Gorman, C. "Sizing Up The Sexes." *Time*, January 20, 1992.

Gregory, A. "Are Women Different and Why Are Women Thought To Be Different? Theoretical and Methodological Perspectives." *Journal of Business Ethics*, 9:257-266, 1990.

Gutfeld, Greg. "Ms. Communication (Miscommunication Between Men and Women In The Workplace)." *Men's Health*, v11n4, p74, May 1996.

Haferd, Laura. "Helping Men, Women Talk To Each Other. Professor Explores The Murky Area Of 'Cross-Gender' Communication In Today's Sexually Charged Workplace." *Beacon Journal* (Akron, OH), Sunday, April 12, 1998.

Hotz, Robert Lee. "Changes in Pregnancy May Boost Brain Power." *Los Angeles Times*, Wednesday, November 11, 1998.

Johnson, K.L. "The Gender Gap: How To Sell the Opposite Sex." *Broker World*, 11:6 June 1991.

Kenton, S.B "Speaker Credibility in Persuasive Business Communication: A Model Which Explains Gender Differences." *The Journal of Business Communication*, 26:2:Spring 1989.

Lusardi, L.A. "When a Woman Speaks, Does Anybody Listen?" *Working Woman*, July 1990.

McCluskey, Karen Curnow. "Gender At Work." *Public Management*, v79n5, p.5. May 1997.

McGinty, Sarah . "How You Speak Shows Where You Rank." *Fortune*, v137n2, PP: 156, February 2, 1998.

Newcombe, N. and Arnkoff, D.B. "Effects of Speech Style and Sex of Speaker on Person Perception." *Journal of Personality and Social Psychology*, Vol ???, No. 8, 1979.

Recer, Paul. "Women Have a More Emotional Memory, Study Finds." *USA Today*, July 23, 2002.

Rosener, J.B. "Ways Women Lead." *Harvard Business Review*, Nov-Dec 1990.

Rubin, Rita. "MRI Scans Confirm That Men Have Half a Mind Not to Listen." *USA Today*, November 29, 2000.

Simons, G. "The Ultimate Cultural Difference – And How To Bridge It." *The International Management Development Review*, Volume Four.

Stewart, Janet Kidd. "Speaking of Differences; How Gender Influences Effective Communication." *Chicago Tribune*, Sunday November 9, 1997.

Sullivan, Andrew. "Why Do Men Act the Way They Do?" Reader's Digest, September 2000, reprinted from *The New York Times Magazine*.

Weisendanger, B. "A Conversation on Conversation With Deborah Tannen." *Sales & Marketing Management*, April 1991.

Zielinski, Dave. "The Gender Gap." *Presentations*, v12n8, pp: 36-42, August 1998.

# ABOUT THE AUTHOR

Jane Sanders is one of the nation's foremost experts on gender communication, both in the workplace and at home.

With Fortune 500 clients nationwide, Jane is a powerful and respected speaker and trainer with over 25 years of successful business experience. Audiences describe her as highly results-oriented, inspirational, down-to-earth, fun, and passionate about her topics.

After earning an MBA, Jane began her successful career with Carnation Company (now Nestlé USA) in sales and marketing. She then managed all sales and marketing efforts with Fortune 500 clients for a prominent international graphic design firm. Jane's enjoyment of and sound success with speeches and presentations propelled her career change to professional speaking and training.

As president of GenderSmart® Solutions, Jane now has a thriving speaking and consulting business on topics that include gender communication, recruiting and retention of women, selling to women, authentic leadership confidence, life and career planning, presentation skills, and strategic planning facilitation. Jane's programs are highly educational, interactive, loaded with easily implementable tips and techniques, and fun.

Jane's clients include MassMutual, Prudential, Thrivent Financial, Ameriprise Financial Services, US Steel, Ford Motor Company, PBS, Anheuser-Busch, Toyota Motor Sales USA, CIGNA, Northrop Grumman, Deloite & Touche, Xerox, Nestlé Foods, Boeing, Hibernia National Bank, and many more companies and associations in the United States and Canada. She is a member of the National Speakers Association and has appeared on radio and television shows to discuss her topics.

To order bulk quantities of GenderSmart®, or for information on Jane's other products and training/consulting services, please call toll free (877) 343-2150 or email Jane@janesanders.com.

# What Jane's clients are saying about her seminars and speeches...

*"Informative and enlightening; truly a learning experience!"*
J. Culver, Nestlé USA

*"I have heard nothing but positive feedback!"*
D. Ruddick, MassMutual

*"You blew them away!"*
A. Edwards, Xerox

*"You received the highest ratings of all sessions!"*
C. Izzi, ABRA

*"Your program was perfect for us!"*
K. Bell, Lexus

*"You were fabulous...nothing but outstanding, positive feedback!"*
T. Shirley, NAEC

*"Engaging, insightful, unique, helpful, fun!"*
J. Wuebben, Ford Motor Company

*"A 10, and I never give 10's!" "A 12 on a 10 scale!"*
Audience members.

*"Your program received rave reviews!"*
B. Labelson, United Way of Los Angeles

*"Your session was rated #1 of all workshops!"*
H. Pankey, IDRC

CPSIA information can be obtained
at www.ICGtesting.com
Printed in the USA
LVHW031537231121
704247LV00012B/1493

9 780972 381024